CW01082026

St. Patrick, his writings and life – Primary Source Edition

Saint Patrick, fl 697 Muirchu maccu Machtheni, Newport J. D. 1860-1936 White

TRANSLATIONS OF CHRISTIAN LITERATURE

SERIES V
LIVES OF THE CELTIC SAINTS
EDITED BY ELEANOR HULL

ST. PATRICK

TRANSLATIONS OF CHRISTIAN LITERATURE

SERIES V
LIVES OF THE CELTIC SAINTS
EDITED BY ELEANOR HULL

ST. PATRICK

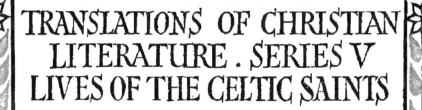

TRANSLATIONS OF CHRISTIAN
LITERATURE . SERIES V
LIVES OF THE CELTIC SAINTS

St. PATRICK
HIS WRITINGS
AND LIFE

By NEWPORT J D WHITE, D·D·

SOCIETY FOR PROMOTING
CHRISTIAN KNOWLEDGE. London
The Macmillan Company . New York

PRINTED IN GREAT BRITAIN BY
RICHARD CLAY & SONS, LIMITED,
BRUNSWICK ST., STAMFORD ST., S.E. 1,
AND BUNGAY, SUFFOLK.

CONTENTS

	PAGE
INTRODUCTION	I
INTRODUCTION TO THE CONFESSION	29
THE CONFESSION	31
INTRODUCTION TO THE LETTER	52
THE LETTER	54
INTRODUCTION TO THE LORICA OF ST. PATRICK	61
THE LORICA OF ST. PATRICK	64
SAYINGS OF PATRICK	67
INTRODUCTION TO MUIRCHU'S LIFE OF ST. PATRICK	68
PREFACE	72
BOOK I	73
BOOK II	102
NOTES ON THE CONFESSION	110
NOTES ON THE LETTER	119
NOTES ON MUIRCHU'S LIFE OF ST. PATRICK	121
INDEX	138

see : J.R. Ardill : St. Patrick A.D. 180 (1931)

7526 A 48

ST. PATRICK

INTRODUCTION

ANY satisfactory answer to the question, Who was St. Patrick, and what did he do? must begin with the two short Latin writings—the Confession and the Letter—the author of which calls himself Patricius, and claims the status of bishop in Ireland.

These documents bear the stamp of genuineness upon them as plainly as does the Epistle of St. Paul to the Galatians or the Second to the Corinthians. If the reader will only take them for what they profess to be—take them at their word—they will repay study as human documents, though they may not constitute any contribution to theology, or make any appeal to the intellect or to the æsthetic faculty.

The first thing to note about them is the fact that the literary criticism of their contents reveals nothing that is inconsistent with the supposition that they were written by a man who lived between A.D. 389 and A.D. 461, the dates of St. Patrick's birth and death according to the most recent calculations.

(A) One of the most striking features in these two short tracts is the number of quotations from the Bible, and the use of Biblical phraseology. The result of an examination of these quotations and phrases is entirely favourable to the hypothesis that the writings belong to the middle of the fifth century. The text of the Latin Bible used is, in the O.T., that current before St. Jerome published his translation from the Hebrew (A.D. 391–404); but the quotations from the N.T., while indicating in a few places the writer's acquaintance with St. Jerome's revision (A.D. 383), exemplify, for the most part, the type of text that was current in Europe before the final triumph of St. Jerome's revision, viz. a mixed text, partly Old Latin and partly Vulgate.

St. Jerome's N.T. came into general use much earlier than did his O.T. Even Muirchu, who wrote about the year 700, has a remarkable quotation from the O.L. of *Exodus*.

The question, as it affects St. Patrick, is dealt with in detail in the present writer's *Libri S. Patricii*, p. 230 ff. But something must be said here.

For the purpose of arriving at a conclusion as to the relation of Patrick's Biblical text to that of Jerome, it is necessary to remember that the Latin Bible is not homogeneous. Of the Psalter, Jerome produced three editions : (1) that called the Roman Psalter (R), A.D. 383, a cursory revision of the Old Latin ; (2) a more careful revision, the Gallican Psalter (G), A.D. 387, which became current in Gaul at the end of the sixth century ; and (3) a new translation from the Hebrew (H). The rest of the canonical books of the O.T. were re-translated by Jerome from the Hebrew (A.D. 391–404) ; but the Apocrypha, with the exception of *Tobit* and *Judith*, he did not touch. The Gospels were carefully revised ; but the evidence as to the rest of the N.T. is conflicting. However, it is generally agreed now that Jerome did revise the Acts, Epistles, and Revelation, but not very thoroughly. Hence we must examine separately Patrick's citations from (1) the Psalter ; (2) the other canonical O T. books ; (3) the Apocrypha ; (4) the Gospels ; and (5) the rest of the N.T.

Moreover, we must keep in mind the fact that no two MSS. of the Vulgate N.T. present an exactly identical text. This lack of uniformity is even more marked in the case of MSS. of the O.L., continuous texts of which are very few in number. Again, it must not be forgotten that Jerome took an O.L. text as the basis of his revision. He did not revise the Acts, Epistles, and Revelation as thoroughly as he had done the Gospels. Consequently, there is always the possibility that any particular rendering in the Vulgate of the Acts, etc., which differs from the often conflicting extant O.L. renderings, may itself be another O.L. rendering, *i. e.* that of the O.L. text used by Jerome and left untouched by him.

Turning now to the analysis of St. Patrick's quotations, we find (1) that of nineteen distinct quotations from the Psalter, seven are cases in which R and G are identical; in ten, Patrick's rendering is that of R or some other O.L. version; in one case Patrick agrees with H, and in one other—Ps. lxix 8, Letter 16—he reads with G, *extraneus,* while one of the two O L. MSS. has *exter,* and the other *alienus.* In both these cases it is highly probable that if there were more O.L. MSS. extant, this H and this G rendering would be found in them. (2) Patrick has seven citations from the canonical O.T., all O.L., some very remarkable ones. (3) He has eleven citations from the Apocrypha. These call for no comment, as here the Vulgate is O.L. It may then be safely said that the text of the O.T. used by Patrick was pre-Hieronymian.

(4) When, however, we turn to the Gospels, while there is a considerable number of O.L. renderings, there are two at least unquestionably from Jerome's revision—viz. the quotation from *Mark* xvi. 15, 16 in Conf. 40, and that of *John* x. 16, in Letter 11. These are sufficient to prove that Patrick was at least acquainted with Jerome's revision of the Gospels. Perhaps the same account is to be given of Patrick's text of the *Acts.* There are three places in which he presents Vulgate readings; but in one case only are the three O.L. MSS. in accord with each other. As regards the Epistles, the most that can be said is that Patrick's is a

mixed Vulgate text; while in the Revelation he agrees always with the O.L. It is noteworthy that some of the renderings found in St. Patrick's Latin writings suggest that he used MSS. emanating from South Gaul. In particular, there are several remarkable readings common to him and the Latin translation of Irenæus. These were noted in my *Libri S. Patricii* and have been collected in Dr. Hitchcock's *Irenæus of Lugdunum*, p. 348 ff.

(B) There are some other points in which these writings reflect the conditions that obtained in the fifth century. The Franks are included in the category of heathen (*gentes*) in Letter 14. In A.D. 496, the Franks, *en masse*, followed their king, Clovis, into the Christian Church.

(C) Again, it has been recently shown that Coroticus, to whose subjects the Letter is addressed, ruled between A.D. 420–450 (Bury, *St. Patrick*, p. 314).

(D) Again, there are polemical allusions to sun-worship in Conf. 20, 60. This was a marked feature in the religion of Mithraism, which was popular all over the Roman Empire during the first four and five centuries of our era.

(E) Again, in these writings Britain is a recognized part of the Roman Empire (Letter 2). The name *Britanniæ*, constantly used, assumes the division of the island into more than one Britain (see note on Conf. 23). The Roman municipal organization is implied in the casual statement that Patrick's father was a *decurio* (Letter 10, where see note). This point, however, does not afford any precise intimation of date. The Roman legions left Britain for the last time in A.D. 410. But there is no reason to think that any one at the time regarded this withdrawal as final. In any case, the forms of Roman civilization, and still more Roman nomenclature, would prevail long after the armed forces of the Empire had withdrawn.

(F) Again, the statement, without comment by Patrick, a bishop and an ascetic, that his father was a deacon and his grandfather a presbyter, certainly reflects an age and a society in which disregard of the rule of celibacy for the secular clergy created no scandal (see the note on Conf. 1).

(G) Again, in two passages of the Letter (2 and 15) the epithet "apostate" is applied to the Picts that were allies of Coroticus. It is not clear why they are called "apostates"; perhaps on account of their having joined Scottic heathen in a raid on Patrick's Scottic Christians; perhaps because of an actual relapse into formal heathenism. In any case, it proves that they had once been Christians. Now St. Ninian's mission to the Southern Picts is dated between A.D. 394 and 432.

The cumulative force of these points is very great, especially when it is remembered that there is no indication in these writings of a later date. Some of the points, moreover, are convincing proofs of the genuineness of the writings. No forger, of the seventh century, say, would have thought it necessary to make Patrick quote from the kind of Biblical text that was current in the fifth century; a forger could scarcely avoid letting fall some remark inconsistent with a date prior to A.D. 461. The only possible motive for the forging of writings under Patrick's name would be to do him honour. But the Confession and the Letter are admirable only from the standpoint of those who recognize the value of the prophet's criterion: "Not by might, nor by power, but by my Spirit, saith the Lord of hosts" (Zech. iv. 6). Apart from his "rusticity" of style, the writer is often unable to express his meaning; the little he does tell us about himself is not easily fitted in with the traditions current in the seventh century; his inconsistent statements—very human and very natural—are not such as a panegyrist would invent for him. And above all, the quality of man revealed in these documents is quite other than the somewhat vindictive saint who was Muirchu's hero, "very impatient of contradiction, and very resentful of injury," as " primitive Irish ecclesiastics, and especially the superior class, commonly known as Saints," are portrayed in the early formal biographies (Reeves, *Adamnan*, p. lxxvii).

The real Patrick, in so far as the presentation to later ages of his personality and work is concerned, has suffered from theory-ridden historians and critics as well as from the partisans of warring sects. With these polemics the present volume does not profess to deal. For a complete refutation of Prof. Zimmer's notion, that Palladius and Patrick were one and the same person, that he was in fact a failure, and dressed up as a success by the Romanizing party in the seventh century, the reader is referred to pp. xcvii.–c. of Dr. Gwynn's edition of the *Book of Armagh*, and to Prof. Bury's *St. Patrick*, p. 384 ff.

It is not proposed in this Introduction to deal with matters which are either plainly stated in St. Patrick's own writings and in Muirchu's Life, or are discussed in the notes There are, however, some questions connected with Patrick which demand separate treatment, and these we shall take in the order suggested by the sequence of events in his career.

We may accept, without discussion, the date, A.D. 389, assigned to his birth by Prof. Bury. His race, birthplace and family are dealt with in the notes on Conf. c. 1.

I

The first historical problem which meets us in connexion with Patrick's personal history concerns the place of his captivity in Ireland This, however, was not a problem at all until the last few years, when literary criticism of the Confession suggested that the Wood of Fochlath—the only Irish place-name in the document—must have been the scene of Patrick's slavery and conversion There is scarcely any point on which Patrician tradition is so constant and unanimous as the identification of the mountain of Conf. 16, on which Patrick spent nights of prayer, with Slemish, in Co. Antrim. On this point the tradition of Ulster is supported by that of Connaught, of Meath and of Leinster.

But, then, how are we to explain Patrick's own words in Conf. 23, where, describing a dream which he had in Britain, between his escape from Ireland and his return thither as a missionary, he says, " I thought that . . . I heard the voice of them who lived beside the Wood of Foclut which is nigh unto the western sea And thus they cried, as with one mouth, We beseech thee, holy youth, to come and walk among us once more"? It is of secondary importance whether we translate *adhuc* "hither" or "once more" (see note *in loc.*); the problem is to explain how Patrick recognized the accent of the natives of the Wood of Fochlath, in Co. Mayo, or even knew the name of the place, if he had never been there.

Patrick's language distinctly implies that the six years of his captivity in Ireland were spent in the service of one man. In my first edition of the *Libri S. Patricii*, I sought a solution of the problem in a supposition that when Patrick escaped from his master, he fled westward, and found the ship of his dreams on the coast of Mayo, at or near Westport. There was an interval of some days—two or more—between his arrival at the port and his sailing. This is suggested by the mention of "the hut where I was lodging" (Conf. 18). He might in that case have had time to become acquainted with the Wood of Fochlath and the speech of its human denizens There are two serious objections to this theory, which I now feel to be fatal (1) A British slave desiring to escape to Britain would run from Slemish in an easterly, or south-easterly direction. (2) It is extremely unlikely that any of the ports of commerce between Ireland and Britain, or Ireland and the Continent, were on the west coast.

Prof. Bury, however, was so much impressed by this passage in the Confession that in his *St. Patrick* he abandoned the Slemish tradition altogether, and asserted that "close to Crochan Aigli, the mount which has been immemorially associated with Patrick's name, the British slave served his master for six years" (*op. cit.* pp. 28, 334 ff.).

It is undoubtedly true that Croagh-Patrick is the greatest Patrician sanctuary in Ireland. Antiquaries visit Slemish; but pilgrims in thousands climb Croagh-Patrick every year for the good of their souls. One of the most picturesque, even sublime, of the Patrician legends is connected with this mountain. It is told in Tirechán's Memoir (fol. 13, v°):—"And Patrick journeyed to Mount Egli to fast on it for forty days and forty nights, observing the discipline of Moses, and of Elijah, and of Christ. . . . And Patrick went forth to the summit of the mountain, over Crochan Aigli, and he stayed there forty days and forty nights. And mighty birds were around him, so that he could not see the face of the sky or earth or sea. For God had said to all the saints of Ireland (past, present and to come): Go up, O ye saints, above the mountain which towers and is higher than all the mountains that are towards the setting of the sun: [Go up] to bless the peoples of Ireland. [This came to pass] that Patrick might see the fruit of his labour; because the company of all the Irish saints came to him, to visit their father."

It must be confessed that Prof. Bury's theory is very attractive; but the only support that it has in antiquity is in the tenth century *Life* by Probus, chap. 29, where Probus, describing the death of Miliucc, as given by Muirchu (i. 12), substitutes "montis Egli" for Muirchu's "montis Miss." This slip of the pen or of the mind—for it is nothing more—is interesting as evidence of the fame of

Croagh-Patrick in the tenth century; but it does not help Prof. Bury's theory very much.

This is a case in which uniform and unbroken tradition may be allowed a decisive voice. No ecclesiastical interest was served by the association of Patrick with Slemish. And, moreover, Tirechán, who was himself a native of Co. Mayo, and deeply interested in the connexion of Patrick with the sacred spots of his district, acquiesces, as Muirchu does, in the claims of Slemish.

How, then, are we to account for Patrick's own words, "I heard the voice of them who lived beside the Wood of Foclut"? I believe that his mission work in Connaught, which was extensive and prolonged, affected his interpretation in old age of the dream he had seen as a young man. The dream occurred about A.D. 414–415 (Bury, *St. Patrick*, p. 338), and the Confession was written towards the close of his career, probably not earlier than A.D. 454. It is no derogation from Patrick's greatness as a "man of God" to say that he had a confused and inaccurate way of thinking. When such a man after forty years recalls a dream, the interpretation thereof is likely to be affected by the actual fulfilment of it. Now the call of the West came to Patrick's ears with a summons as compelling as the call of the East has been to later missionaries. Twice he emphasizes the fact that he had "preached to the limit beyond which no man dwells" (Conf. 34, 51). Tirechán records (fol. 15 r° b) that "Patrick crossed the Shannon three times, and spent seven years on the western shore." When these facts are taken into consideration, it will not be thought unreasonable to suppose that what had been, when first heard, a call from Ireland generally came to be thought of, quite naturally, as a call from the people dwelling under the great "Hill of the Eagle," the sight of which has always impressed the imagination.

It is fair to say, on the other hand, that the story

(preserved by Tirechán, fol. 10, v° *a*) of how Patrick came to visit the Wood of Fochlath in the first instance, assumes that at the time when Patrick saw the dream, the name "Wood of Fochlath" was divinely communicated to him. Tirechán says that when Patrick was at Tara the second time, "two noblemen were conversing behind his back; and one said to the other . . . Tell me thy name, I pray thee, and that of thy father, and of thy farm, and of thy plain, and where thy house is. And he replied, I am Endeus, the son of Amolngid, the son of Fechrach, the son of Echach; from the western shores, from the plain of Domnon, and from the Wood of Fochloth. Now when Patrick heard the name of the Wood of Fochloth, he rejoiced greatly, and said to Endeus the son of Amolngid, I too will go with thee, if I am alive, because the Lord bade me go. And Endeus said, Thou shalt not go with me, lest we both be killed. Then the Saint said, Of a truth thou too shalt never reach thy country alive, if I come not with thee, nor shalt thou have eternal life; because for my sake thou didst come hither, as Joseph [was sent into Egypt] before the children of Israel. . . . And they undertook a journey to Mount Egli . . . because necessity required of them that they should reach the Wood of Fochlith before the crown of the year, the second Easter [in Ireland], because he had heard the voices of children crying with great outcry in the womb of their mothers, and saying, Come, holy Patrick, to save us."

The simple and probable dream of the Confession has in this version "suffered a theological change into something weird and strange," a suggestive illustration of the growth of legend out of truth. But apart from that, the story of Tirechán is at least proof that the Connaught tradition was that Patrick had never been in the Fochlath district until he came there as a missionary, and that Patrick's dream was believed to be a supernatural revelation

of a place-name hitherto unknown to him.   Patrick himself,
too, may have so conceived of it; but he does not plainly
say so.   In any case, the solution which I have offered is
psychologically probable.

II

What did Patrick do in the years between his escape
from the sailors, A.D. 411 or 412, and his consecration as
bishop in A.D. 432?   The Confession (c. 43) implies that
he spent some years at least in Gaul; that was his spiritual
home: his heart's desire was "to go as far as Gaul, in order
to visit the brethren and to behold the face of the saints of
my Lord."   But the first of the *Dicta Patricii*, preserved in
the *Book of Armagh* (fol. 9 r° *a*) gives slightly more detailed
information:—"I had the fear of God as the guide of my
journey through Gaul and Italy and, moreover, in the islands
which are in the Tyrrhene Sea."   "Italy," in this Saying,
need not mean anything farther than the districts of Italy
adjacent to Gaul.   Tírechán states (fol. 9 r° *b*) that Patrick
spent seven years in these wanderings.   He quotes the
Dictum as made by Patrick "in commemoratione laborum."
I take the Saying to be in itself the *commemoratio laborum;*
there is no need to postulate a book with that title.
Tírechán adds, on the authority of Bishop Ultan, that "he
was for thirty years in one of those islands, which is called
Aralanensis [Lérins]."   This is all that Tírechán tells us
about Patrick's non-Irish career; he says nothing about
Auxerre or Germanus; Muirchu, on the other hand, says
nothing about Lérins.

We can affirm with much more confidence that Patrick
studied at Lérins, the great monastery recently founded by
St. Honoratus, than that he "read the Canon with Germanus" at Auxerre.   The statement in the Saying is
supported, as has been already mentioned, by the fact that

B

the few indications of *provenance* supplied by the text of
Patrick's Biblical quotations point to Southern Gaul. In
all likelihood Patrick's studies were almost wholly Biblical
and devotional. He certainly did read the Commentary
on the Apocalypse by Victorinus of Pettau (see notes on
Conf. 4 and 14); and Dr. F. R. Montgomery Hitchcock
has pointed out (*Irenæus of Lugdunum*, p. 348 ff.) many
resemblances in style between Patrick and the Latin
Irenæus. Again, Patrick's version of Mal. iv. 2, 3 is identical with that found in the *De Civitate Dei*. But this need
mean no more than the use of similar Biblical texts by
St. Augustine and St Patrick. There is no reflection in
Patrick's writings of the theological controversies which
were occupying the minds of his intellectual contemporaries;
and it is probable that his deficiency in this respect con-
stituted one of the objections urged by his *seniores* against
his undertaking missionary work in Ireland (Conf. 37, 46).
It will be remembered that at this period the Pelagian
heresy was agitating the Church in Britain, and perhaps in
Ireland too.

"After a few years" (Conf. 23) passed in Lérins, Patrick
returned to Britain, and here the call of the West came to
him with insistence. The date assigned to this visit to
Britain (A.D 414 or 415), by Professor Bury seems to allow
only three years for his stay at Lérins, which appears too
short. On the other hand, if there is any basis of fact in
Muirchu's confused references to Bishop Amator, Patrick
must have gone to Auxerre not later than A.D. 418, in which
year Amator died.

Nothing can be affirmed with certainty as to the happenings of the period A.D. 418–432. The language of the
Confession implies three occasions on which Patrick was
the object of adverse criticism. (1) We may suppose that
c. 46 ("Many were forbidding this embassage, etc.")
refers to the time when Patrick first mooted the notion of

a mission to Ireland. Then (2) there came an attack in Britain (c. 32), when Patrick's "dearest friend" fought for him in his absence. And finally (3), the deadliest blow of all (cc. 26-33), when "not a few of his elders," supported by his quondam dearest friend, "came and urged his sins against his laborious episcopate."

I would venture to suggest that these dim hints possibly indicate that Patrick's evangelizing work in Ireland, as distinguished from his work as bishop, began before the year 432. In the first place, it is difficult to see what ground Patrick could have given the *seniores* for their second attack, if he had not *done* something to irritate them. Again, unlearned as he was, Patrick must have given Germanus some proof of his powers to justify his consecration as missionary bishop, at once, on the death of Palladius.

It is tempting to identify Patrick's "dearest friend" with Germanus himself. In c. 32 he says, "He himself had said to me with his own lips, Lo, thou art to be raised to the rank of bishop . . . an office which . . . he had of his own accord and gladly conceded to me." This language strongly suggests that the friend was also the consecrating bishop. Again, if we suppose, as is most probable, that the third attack was made in Britain, the date of Germanus second visit to Britain, A.D. 447, would fit in exactly with the data supplied by the Confession. The attack was made, Patrick says, "after the lapse of thirty years." He does not say whether he is reckoning from the date of the sinful act, or from the date of the confession of it. If we adopt the latter alternative, we have the year 417 as the date of the confession—that is, about the year when Patrick was ordained deacon (or priest) by Bishop Amator, according to Prof. Bury's calculation.

The truth or falsity of this theory depends on the truth or falsity of Muirchu's statement that Patrick received orders of some kind from Amator. What Muirchu actually says is that Patrick was consecrated bishop by Amator. As this is obviously absurd, Prof. Bury naturally concludes that Amator ordained Patrick deacon. If this supposition—and it is no more—be correct, it is extremely unlikely that Germanus could have been Patrick's bosom friend at that time; for up to the year 418 Germanus was a layman of very exalted rank. On the other hand, it must be remembered that Muirchu is the only ancient source-authority for any connexion between Amator and Patrick, and his account of the matter is, at best, confused and inaccurate. Moreover, the introduction of Amator into the story compels us to assume that Patrick spent not more than three years at Lérins, which is both utterly at variance with the most ancient tradition (the evidence of Ultan), and also in itself unlikely. We need not press the "thirty years" of Conf. 26 too nicely; it is evidently a round number and occurs in a statement in which the writer was not likely to underestimate the length of the interval. If Amator be eliminated from the history, the supposition that Germanus conferred on Patrick all the Holy Orders will not seem unreasonable. If the great Germanus were Patrick's false friend, the suppression of the name by Patrick in the Confession would be most natural.

III

The mention of St. Patrick's consecration as missionary bishop in Ireland naturally suggests two further questions: Who sent him? and, To whom was he sent?—that is, Were they a wholly heathen people? The first question may be answered simply by saying that Patrick was sent to Ireland by the Church of the Roman Empire. In order to a common-sense examination of this matter, we must, as far as is possible, get back mentally into the fifth century, and forget the later antagonisms which the growing pretensions of Rome—then in an early if vigorous stage—called into existence.

What do we learn from Patrick himself on this subject? " I am a bishop, appointed by God, in Ireland " (Letter 1). But for St. Patrick, as for St. Paul, the source-authority of God is in harmony with the agent-authority of the Church ; and in Patrick's mind the Church of the Empire was the only Church of the only civilized human society.   The term *Romani* occurs twice in the Letter (cc. 2 and 14) ; in both places it is equivalent to *civilized Christians*. When St. Patrick wrote, the Empire had been nominally Christian for more than a hundred years, and had also, for centuries previously, been practically conterminous with civilization, at least from the standpoint of its subjects.   And this association of Christianity and civilization became more and more intimately connected with the Roman Empire, as the presence all around of the heathen barbarians forced itself increasingly on the notice of its citizens.   It is difficult for us now to realize what Rome—imperial, civilized, Christian—meant to those who in the fourth or fifth centuries styled themselves *Romani*.   Even though the Roman legions had withdrawn from Britain finally, as it proved to be, about the year 410, yet in Britain, no less than nearer the centre, Rome long remained more than " the shadow of a great name " ; it stood for the highest, perhaps the only conceivable, form of ordered society ; its efface-ment was unthinkable.   The phrase " The Holy Roman Empire" expresses one of the ideals in which St. Patrick lived.   This grand conception underlies his use of the term *Romani*.

This proved connotation of the word in the Letter is the key to the interpretation of one of the *Dicta Patricii* (Book of Armagh, fol. 9 r° *a*) : "Ecclesia Scotorum, immo Romanorum, ut Christiani ita ut Romani sitis, ut decantetur uobiscum oportet omni hora orationis uox illa laudabilis *Curie lession. Christe lession.* Onnis ecclesia quæ sequitur me cantet *Cyrie lession, Christe lession.*" "Church of the Irish! nay, of the Romans! In order that ye be Christians as well as Romans ye must chant in your churches at every hour of prayer that glorious word, *Kyrie eleison, Christe eleison,* etc."

Whatever may be the decision of liturgical experts as to the genuineness of the second part of the Saying, the first part has in it a true Patrician ring. It is no mere meticulous rubric ; it is a clarion call to Irish Christians to come out of provincialism into imperialism in religion. In this Saying we hear Patrick, "the traveller and the Roman citizen," scouting the insular prejudices of "the Irish believing in Christ," to whom he had been sent as an organizing apostle, with a mission to bring the island lying just outside civilization into line with Christendom.

As regards the connexion of the Bishop of Rome with Patrick's mission, it is, on the one hand, true that Pope Celestine, by consecrating Palladius for Ireland in A.D. 431, initiated the work which Patrick, as the successor to Palladius, began, as bishop at least, in A.D. 432. But all the really ancient evidence is against the notion that Celestine was consulted about Patrick's consecration. Muirchu states that as soon as the death of Palladius was reported in Gaul, Patrick was without delay consecrated and despatched to Ireland by Germanus of Auxerre. Tirechán says nothing whatever about the matter ; but his silence, and the positive evidence of Muirchu, are all the more significant when it is remembered that they both belonged to the then Romanizing party in the Irish Church. But St. Patrick's own silence on the subject is the most illuminating fact of all. He wrote his Confession—his *Apologia pro vita sua*—to vindicate his action in having come to Ireland at all. His appeal is altogether to the Divine call and the Divine blessing on his work. Patrick, as a fifth-century Christian, shared, of course, in the veneration and deference then paid to the Bishop of Rome—the deference given, not the deference claimed. The Pope's sanction, if it had been expressly given, would surely have counted for much even in the estimation of the remote Christians of Britain and of Ireland. The note in the Book of Armagh (fol. 16 r° *a*), which states that "Bishop Patrick was sent to teach the Irish by Bishop Celestine, the Pope of Rome," has been proved conclusively by Dr. Gwynn to be a note of the scribe Ferdomnach (A.D. 807–846) and not part of the Memoir of Tirechán.

There is a statement by Tirechán (fol. 9 r° *a*) which implies his belief that St. Patrick paid a visit to Rome some years after his consecration: "A compassionate man [in Roscommon] . . named Hercaith . . . believed in the God of Patrick; and Patrick baptized him, and his son Feradachus. And he dedicated his son to Patrick, and he went forth with Patrick to study for thirty years, and he ordained him in the city of Rome, and gave him a new name, Sachellus, and he wrote for him a Psalter which I have seen, and he carried thence a portion of the relics of Peter and Paul, of Laurence and Stephen, which are in Armagh." Prof. Bury (*St. Patrick*, p. 367) brings this passage into relation with an entry in the Ulster Annals, *sub. an.* 441. "Leo ordinatus est xlii. Romane ecclesie episcopus, et probatus est in fide Catolica Patricius episcopus." Prof. Bury supposes that Patrick went to Rome in the early years of Leo's pontificate, and received Papal approval of his work. This is an ingenious and plausible theory. Against it must be set the fact that Muirchu plainly knew nothing of such a visit; for he tells us (i. 5. 6.) of Patrick's *desire* to go to Rome, but that he went no further than Gaul. The Confession was almost certainly written after A.D. 441. Its silence about the Pope is significant. It is reasonable to argue that if St. Patrick had taken the trouble to go

to seek the Pope's blessing, he would have valued it
sufficiently to adduce it in a written defence of his
conduct.

IV

The second question raised by the mention of Patrick's
consecration is, Was his projected work in Ireland wholly
among heathen peoples?

Every reader of the New Testament knows that there
were Christians in Rome before St. Paul went thither "to
impart to them some spiritual gift to the end that they
might be established"; and yet early Christian writers
express the truth when they speak of the Church of Rome
as having been founded by St. Peter and St. Paul. That
is to say, it was by the ministry of those Apostles that the
various congregations of Christians in the city of Rome
were given a definite organization, made a church, brought
into line with the earlier organized churches of Jerusalem,
Antioch, Ephesus, Corinth, etc.

In exactly the same way St. Patrick founded the Church
in Ireland. He was the instrument by means of which
the scattered Christians in Ireland, individuals and small
communities, chiefly in the South, were brought into
touch, as an organized church, with the rest of Western
Christendom.

The problem involved may be put in another way thus:
Among the differences in externals between Celtic Christianity and that of the Continent there were two which
were considered important, viz., the mode of calculating
the incidence of Easter, and the form of the clerical
tonsure. The controversy was settled, as far as Britain
was concerned, at the Synod of Whitby, A.D. 664, when
the Continental party triumphed. The struggle naturally
continued longer in Ireland—about fifty years, in fact.

The question, then, is: Did Patrick, in his presentation

of the faith to the Irish people, introduce into Ireland these Celtic peculiarities? or, Were they in Ireland before he came, as characteristics of the sporadic Christianity already existing there, and prevalent to such a degree that he was either unable to suppress them, or unwilling to make the attempt—unwilling, that is, to divert his energies from the work of evangelization to polemics?

We are compelled to accept the second alternative. Many considerations combine to prove that Christianity had a footing in Ireland before the fifth century. It came, as elsewhere, with commerce. Although Ireland was not included in the Roman Empire, it was from the earliest times in touch with Britain and the Continent of Europe. Even if we had not the famous note of Prosper of Aquitaine, *s.a.* 431, "Ad Scottos in Christum credentes. . . . Palladius primus episcopus mittitur," we have positive, if indirect, evidence of the existence of a pre-Patrician Christianity: (1) Prof. Zimmer has shown (*Early Celtic Church*, pp. 24–26) that some Christian technical terms—as, for example, *Trinity, altar, candle, presbyter*—have in Irish forms which prove that they were not borrowed directly from the Latin, but came through the British language. (2) Again, it is plain from passages in St. Patrick's Confession (*e.g.* cc. 47, 50–54) that amongst his detractors were Irish Christians, the same, doubtless, to whom he refers in one of his Sayings as calling themselves *ecclesia Scotorum.* (3) Again, while Patrick's language, if accepted without qualification, implies that Ireland was wholly heathen before his arrival (*e. g.* Conf. 41), yet Conf. 51 implies that there had been other Christian preachers in the island who yet had not penetrated as far as he had done: "I journeyed . . . to outlying regions . . . where never had any one come to baptize, or ordain clergy, or confirm the people." (4) Again, it is significant that the early records, when they go into details, speak almost wholly of St.

Patrick's missionary labours in the north and west of Ireland. Tirechán's itinerary leaves off abruptly when Patrick reaches Cashel. This may be explained by the sudden death of the author, or by the loss of leaves from the exemplar which Ferdomnach copied; but it may also be due to the fact that Tirechán was unable to obtain any further record of Patrick's work in Munster. And, moreover, the practical limitation of his sphere of influence to the north of Ireland is indicated by his choice of Armagh as the seat of his ecclesiastical jurisdiction (see Bury, *St. Patrick*, p. 160 ff.).

Now although Patrick was a British Celt by birth, his education, especially his theological and ecclesiastical education, had been imparted to him in Gaul, at Lérins and at Auxerre. It is quite inconceivable that Patrick should have thought about the Paschal question and the tonsure differently from his Gallic preceptors and fellow-students, "the saints of the Lord," whose faces he so earnestly longed to see once more as he felt the approach of death. We can, moreover, account the more easily for Patrick's acquiescence in the Irish peculiarities when we remember that during his lifetime the burning question in the Western Church was not uniformity in ecclesiastical order and discipline, but the great doctrinal and philosophical Pelagian controversy about freewill and original sin.

Prof. Bury, in appraising the "eminent significance" of Patrick in history, observes that "he did three things: he organized the Christianity which already existed; he converted kingdoms which were still pagan, especially in the west; and he brought Ireland into connexion with the Church of the Empire, and made it formally part of universal Christendom" (*St. Patrick*, p. 212). As one of the means to this end, he "diffused a knowledge of Latin in Ireland" (*ib.* p. 217). He did not introduce the Latin

language into Ireland. This had been done by the unknown
pre-Patrician missionaries who were responsible for the
copies of the Old Latin Gospels, etc., which Patrick must
have found on his arrival. But the constant entry in
Tirechán of how at various centres Patrick *scripsit elementa,*
or *scripsit abgitorium* (= *abcedarium*), *i.e.* taught the elements
of learning, indicates the prevalence of the tradition that
the learning for which Ireland afterwards became famous
owed its inception to him.

If Patrick was not himself a learned man, he appreciated
the value of learning. Perhaps, relatively to the standard
of his age and native land, he was not very deficient in
this respect. In any case, it is as a Christian leader that
his measure must be taken. He planted great ideals in
a new soil; and the value of this achievement is not
impaired, so far as the planter is concerned, if the nature
of the soil was prejudicial to a rapid or healthy growth.
The mere presence of ideals, when it is recognized, is in
itself a moral revolution. The man or the nation that has
once seen a vision can never again be as before. I have
elsewhere characterized St. Patrick as a man of apostolic
quality and Pauline temperament. Immeasurably inferior
to St Paul in knowledge and in intellect, he was his equal
in the completeness of his self-consecration to the service
of Christ; and in that lay the secret of his success in life
and of the attraction of his personality after death. He
"was not disobedient unto the heavenly vision"; and his
constant application to himself of the language which
St. Paul uses when speaking of his personal relations to
God, to his work, his converts and his adversaries, does
not strike the reader as presumptuous or ridiculous, because
we feel that it is justified by St. Patrick's moral and
spiritual kinship with the Apostle of the Gentiles.

The amount of literature dealing with St. Patrick is

enormous; and it would be useless and confusing to attempt here to set out a complete bibliography. The following list of fundamental authorities will, it is thought, be sufficient to set the student in the right direction and enable him to find his way for himself in the fascinating bypaths of Patrician lore.

1. One of the very early, if not the earliest, of the documents illustrative of the life of St. Patrick is the Hymn *in laudem S. Patricii* ascribed to St. Sechnall or Secundinus, "the first hymn that was made in Ireland," according to the ancient Irish Preface.

The Annals of Ulster state that Sechnall died in his 75th year on the 27th November, A.D. 447. If this date be accepted, the Hymn would probably be earlier than St. Patrick's own Latin writings, which seem to have been composed in his old age. Whoever composed it, "this hymn is undoubtedly contemporary" (Bury, *St. Patrick,* p. 117). Patrick is spoken of as though he were still alive; and although the eulogy is extravagant, no miracles, save those of the grace of God, are ascribed to him. The Biblical quotations, few in all, point to the use of an Old Latin text, whereas St. Patrick exhibits in some places acquaintance with the Vulgate New Testament.

If the entry in the Ulster Annals mentioned above be correct, it is impossible that Sechnall could have succeeded Patrick in the See of Armagh, as some early lists attest (see Todd, *St. Patrick,* p. 174 ff. and H. J Lawlor, *The Ancient List of the Coarbs of Patrick, Proc. R.I.A.,* xxxv. C. 9); and it is not likely that he was Patrick's sister's son, as is affirmed in the Irish Prefaces to the Hymn. Sechnall is mentioned by Tirechán in a list of bishops consecrated in Ireland by Patrick, and his name is preserved in that of a place in Co. Meath, Dunshaughlin, *i.e.* Domnach Sechnall, Sechnall's Church. It is there that the Hymn is said to have been composed.

According to the Irish Preface, Sechnall wrote it to make his peace with Patrick, who was displeased at a remark of Sechnall's that was reported to him : "A good man were Patrick, were it not for one thing, viz., that he preaches charity so little." When Sechnall recited the Hymn to Patrick, the latter was so well pleased with it, that, after some bargaining in spiritual values, he said to its author, "Thou shalt have this boon: every one who shall recite it at lying down and rising up shall go to heaven." "I accept that," said Sechnall, "but the hymn is long, and not everyone will be able to commit it to memory." "Its grace," said Patrick, "shall be on the last three capitula." "*Deo Gratias*," said Sechnall.

One of the Four Honours due to Patrick in all the monasteries and churches of Ireland (Book of Armagh, fol. 16 r° *a*) is that "his hymn should be sung during the whole time [three days and three nights] of his festival." "His hymn" means the hymn in praise of him. In accordance with this it is entitled in the MS., *Ymnus Sancti Patricii.*

The hymn itself consists of twenty-three quatrains, corresponding to the letters of the alphabet; the first word of each quatrain begins with a different letter (*Audite, Beata, Constans*, etc.). Although this hymn does not supply a single detail respecting St. Patrick's history, its historical value is considerable in view of doubts that have been raised as to Patrick's existence and identity. The hymn is a most impressive witness alike to the success of Patrick's missionary work in Ireland and to the veneration which his consistent Christian life inspired. As a specimen we may quote two stanzas :—

III

Steadfast in the fear of God, and in faith unshaken
Upon him, as upon Peter, the Church is built.
His apostleship he hath received from God.
Against him the gates of hell prevail not.

XXI

Christ chose him for Himself to be His vicar on earth,
Who from twofold slavery doth set captives free ;
Of whom very many he redeems from slavery to men,
Countless numbers he releases from the dominion of the devil.

A critical edition of St. Sechnall's Hymn will be found in *The Irish Liber Hymnorum*, edited in 1898, for the Henry Bradshaw Society, by J. H. Bernard, D.D., and R. Atkinson, LL.D. It has been edited separately, with translation and notes, in 1918, by the Rev. G. F. Hamilton, Rector of Moylough, Co. Galway.

2. Of the *extant* documents, excepting St. Patrick's own writings, the next in point of antiquity is the Memoir of Bishop Tirechán, preserved in the Book of Armagh (fol. 9 r°–fol. 15 v° *b*). This was written not earlier than A.D. 664, possibly about A.D. 670. Tirechán indicates in his Memoir that he was a native of Tirawley in the Co. Mayo, and that his information was derived mainly from Ultan, bishop of Ardbraccan, in Meath, whose pupil he was. Ultan died in A.D. 657. From him Tirechán derived written and oral information about Patrick ; and he also consulted other *seniores*. The book in Ultan's keeping (*Liber apud Ultanum*) would be the earliest attempt to give an account of Patrick of which we have any knowledge. Tirechán's Memoir thus embodies the traditions of Meath and of Connaught.

The avowed purpose of Tirechán's work was to set forth, primarily for the men of Meath, a formal record of the sphere of authority of the See of Armagh, the *paruchia Patricii*, as against the rival claims and encroachments of other religious centres in Ireland. This is done by an enumeration, in the form of an itinerary, of all the churches founded, and clergy appointed, by Patrick. Book I. deals with churches alleged to have been founded in the first year of Patrick's mission, mostly in Meath and Longford.

Book II. brings "him across the Shannon . . . through Connaught; thence into Western and Northern Ulster, briefly indicating his course from Donegal to Antrim—but with no mention of Down, and only a passing word possibly implying a visit of the Saint to Armagh. . . . Then comes the Saint's return to Meath; followed by a very brief note of his move southward to Leinster, and thence to Cashel, at which point the Book breaks off abruptly, perhaps incomplete " (Dr. Gwynn, *Book of Armagh*, p. xlvi.). The lists of names are interspersed with stories connected with the various places, derived from Irish legendary sources, poetical as well as prose. Many of these narrative pieces are more striking and picturesque than anything in the Life by Muirchu. Translations of some of them will be found in the notes. A characteristic feature of Tirechán's work is an attempt to give accurate chronological data. The Memoir produces on the reader the impression of an honest author who had no gift of composition, but who set down faithfully the facts that he deemed relative to his proposed object. The work everywhere assumes on the part of his readers familiarity with the history of St. Patrick; so that it is not always safe to use the silence of Tirechán as an argument adverse to alleged happenings.

3. Of the Life by Muirchu, an account will be found in the Preface to the translation, p. 68.

4. The hymn called, from its opening words, *Genair Patraicc*, is also known as "St. Fiace's Hymn." Fiace the Fair (*albus*) was a poet, and pupil of Dubthach, an eminent poet at Tara when Patrick visited it. Fiace was consecrated by Patrick first bishop of Slebte (Sletty) in Co. Carlow. The hymn itself, by its references to *written* sources, is proved not to be the work of a contemporary. The date assigned to it by modern critics is about A.D. 800. A critical edition of it will be found in the *Irish Liber*

Hymnorum (i. 96 ff., ii. 31 ff., 175 ff.). See also Bury (*St. Patrick*, p. 263 ff.). The hymn is in Irish, and, unlike the work of St. Sechnall, it is full of details about Patrick's life. Of the thirty-four couplets printed fifteen only belong to the original poem, according to recent literary criticism.

5. A collection of seven ancient Lives of St. Patrick was published at Louvain in 1647 by John Colgan, S.J., in his *Trias Thaumaturga*. As reference is commonly made to some of them in accordance with Colgan's notation, it will be convenient to enumerate them here.

Vita I. The hymn *Genair Patraicc*. See above, No. 4.

Vita II. Incomplete; compiled by an Irishman.

Vita III. "Dating perhaps from the ninth century." Prof. Bury published a critical edition of this *Vita*, in 1903, in *Transactions of R.I.A.*, xxxii. C. 3.

Vita IV. Compiled by some one who was ignorant of Irish.

Vita V. By one Probus, of whom nothing else is known. Colgan reprinted this Life from the Basel edition of Bede's work, 1563. The date of this compilation is "hardly much earlier than the middle of the tenth century" (see Bury, *St. Patrick*, p. 273).

Vita VI. By Jocelin, a monk of Furness; twelfth century.

Vita VII. This is usually cited as the *Vita Tripartita*; so named by Colgan, because it is divided into three parts. It is written in Irish, interspersed with Latin phrases and passages. Colgan's edition is a Latin translation of the Irish. The first edition of the Irish text is that published, with other Patrician documents, in the Rolls Series, by Dr. Whitley Stokes, in 1887. This Life was originally compiled about the ninth century, but assumed its present form in the eleventh (see Bury, *St. Patrick*, p. 269 ff.). My references to the Tripartite Life are to Stokes' edition.

Vitæ II, IV and V are largely based on Muirchu. Prof. Bury has demonstrated that *Vitæ* II and IV are based on a compilation, named by him W, which was based on Muirchu (The Tradition of Muirchu's Text, *Hermathena*, xxviii.).

6. The *Book of Armagh*, to which constant reference must be made, is a MS. preserved in the library of Trinity College, Dublin, written sometime between A.D. 807 and A.D. 846, by Ferdomnach, the official scribe of Armagh. The edition of this MS, published for the Royal Irish Academy in 1913 by Dr. John Gwynn, Regius Professor of Divinity in the University of Dublin, is indispensable to serious students of St. Patrick's history. The present writer owes more to this work and to its gracious and learned author than he can express in words. The contents of the MS are as follows :—(1) Life by Muirchu, (2) *Dicta Patricii*, (3) Memoir by Tirechán, (4) Three Petitions of Patrick, (5) Five notes by the scribe, (6) Records derived from the archives of Armagh respecting certain Patrician foundations in Meath, Connaught and Leinster, (7) More notes by the scribe about Patrick, (8) *Liber Angeli* (an imaginative work in support of the claims of Armagh), (9) An imperfect copy of St. Patrick's Confession, (10) A complete copy of the Celtic text of the Vulgate New Testament, known as D in Textual Criticism, and (11) The Life of St. Martin by Sulpicius Severus.

7. Documents (1) to (8) were published with Latin notes, and the readings of the Brussels MS. of Muirchu's Life, in 1882, in *Analecta Bollandiana*, by the Rev. Edmund Hogan, S.J. This work is of great value.

8, 9 Of modern historians of St. Patrick two stand out of pre-eminent merit :—James Henthorn Todd, and John Bagnell Bury. Dr. Todd's *St. Patrick, Apostle of Ireland : a Memoir of his Life and Mission*, Dublin, 1864, is a thesaurus of all that had been up to that date written or conjectured about the Saint. In some respects his

C

work has not been superseded by the more brilliant and profound critical labours of Prof. Bury, whose book, *The Life of St. Patrick, and his Place in History*, appeared in 1905.

10. A critical edition of St. Patrick's Confession and Letter, based on all the known MSS., was published a few months before Prof. Bury's book, by the present writer, under the title of *Libri Sancti Patricii*, in *Proceedings R.I.A.*, xxv. C. 7, and a revised Latin text with a selection of various readings was published in 1918, by the S.P.C.K.

11. A collection of ecclesiastical canons attributed to St. Patrick will be found in Haddan and Stubbs' *Councils*, ii. 328 ff., and in Wasserschleben's *Die Irische Kanonensammlung*. The genuineness of these canons has been vehemently disputed. Prof. Bury is at great pains to vindicate them (*St. Patrick*, p. 233 ff.) It is antecedently probable that Patrick of Armagh, in conjunction with Auxilius and Iserninus of Leinster, drew up a body of disciplinary canons for the regulation of the communities administered by them, and that these canons are in the collection now extant; but canons easily lend themselves to later interpolations and additions; and it would be rash to accept the collection in its entirety as Patrician.

INTRODUCTION TO THE CONFESSION

[Those who desire notes, exegetical and critical, on the Latin text are referred to the edition of the *Libri Sancti Patricii*, published by the Royal Irish Academy in 1905 (*Proceedings*, xxv. C. 7), and to the revised critical text, published in 1918 by the S.P.C.K.]

THE title *Confession* as applied to the first of St. Patrick's writings, in the cognate MSS. C, F₃, F₄, must have been suggested by his own words in cc. 61, 62, "I shall briefly set forth the words of my confession." . . . "This is my confession before I die." But *confession* has not here any penitential association; it is an open and thankful acknowledgment of the goodness of God. The verb *confiteor* is thus used in cc. 3, 4, 5, as frequently in the Vulgate Psalter: "I thank him who hath enabled me in all things, because he did not hinder me from the journey on which I had resolved, and from my labour which I had learnt from Christ my Lord (c. 30)." As addressed to men, the Confession is an *Apologia pro vita sua*. But in Patrick's mind his life was summed up in one fact, viz., his mission work in Ireland, and that not in its details, but in its net spiritual result. He wrote with two classes of readers in his mind: his "kinsfolk" in Britain, who for the most part opposed and depreciated him, and his "sons" in Ireland. For these latter the Confession was intended as "a legacy," "to strengthen and confirm their faith" (cc. 14, 47). Patrick probably never felt himself at home in Ireland; he was "bound in the Spirit" to remain there till his death, and he was faithful unto death to the charge laid upon him by God; but his mind was often in Britain as he was writing (see, *e.g.*, Conf. 42: "Those of *our* race who are born *there*").

The earliest title of the two tracts—Confession and Letter— is that found in the Book of Armagh, *Libri Sancti Patricii*. *Liber* is also found in the colophon of C F₃ F₄. B has, *Incipit vita beati Patricii*. This is perhaps suggested by *Vita* IV, 16, in which Conf. 16 is cited as *in libro quem de uita et conversatione ejus ipse conscripsit*. Another title is *Libri Epistolarum*, found in *Vitæ* III, IV, *Trip.*

CONFESSION

[As far as possible, in the quotations from the Bible, which are printed in italics, the rendering of the English Version of 1611 has been followed, except in O.T. Apocrypha, in which the Douay Version of 1609 has been used.]

1. I, Patrick the sinner, am the most illiterate and the least of all the faithful, and contemptible in the eyes of very many.

My father was Calpurnius, a deacon, one of the sons of Potitus, a presbyter, who belonged to the village of Banavem Taberniæ. Now he had a small farm hard by, where I was taken captive.

I was then about sixteen years of age. I knew not the true God; and I went into captivity to Ireland with many thousands of persons, according to our deserts, because we departed away from God, and kept not his commandments, and were not obedient to our priests, who used to admonish us for our salvation. And the Lord *poured upon* us *the fury of his anger*,[1] and scattered us amongst many heathen, even *unto the ends of the earth*,[2] where now my littleness may be seen amongst men of another nation.

2. And there the Lord *opened the understanding*[3] of my unbelief that, even though late, I might call my faults to remembrance, and that I might *turn with all my heart*[4] to the Lord my God, who *regarded* my *low estate*,[5] and pitied the youth of my ignorance, and kept me before I knew him, and before I had discernment or could distinguish

---

[1] Isa. xlii. 25.   [2] Acts xiii. 47.   [3] Luke xxiv. 45.
[4] Joel ii. 12.   [5] Luke i. 48.

between good and evil, and protected me and comforted me as a father does his son.

3. Wherefore then I cannot keep silence—nor would it be fitting—concerning such great benefits and such great grace as the Lord hath vouchsafed to bestow on me in the land of my captivity; because this is what we can render unto him, namely, that after we have been chastened, and have come to the knowledge of God, we shall exalt and *praise his wondrous works*[1] before *every nation which is under the whole heaven* [2]

4. Because there is no other God, nor was there ever any in times past, nor shall there be hereafter, except God the Father unbegotten, without beginning, from whom all things take their beginning, holding all things [*i. e.*, Almighty], as we say, and his Son Jesus Christ, whom we affirm verily to have always existed with the Father before the creation of the world, with the Father after the manner of a spiritual existence, begotten ineffably before the beginning of anything. And *by him* were made *things visible and invisible.*[3]   He was made man ; and having overcome death, he was received up into heaven to the Father. And *he gave to him all power above every name of things in heaven and things in earth and things under the earth ; and let every tongue confess to him that Jesus Christ is Lord and God*[4] in whom we believe.   And we look for his coming soon to be ; he the Judge of the quick and the dead, *who will render to every man according to his deeds.*[5]   And *he shed on us abundantly the Holy Ghost,*[6] the gift and earnest of immortality, who makes those who believe and obey to become *children of God* the Father and *joint heirs with Christ,*[7] whom we confess and adore as one God in the Trinity of the Holy Name.

---

[1] Ps. lxxxix. 5.   [2] Acts ii. 5.   [3] Col. i. 16.
[4] Phil. ii. 9–11   [5] Rom. ii. 6.
[6] Tit. iii. 5, 6.   .   [7] Rom. viii. 16, 17.

5. For he himself hath said through the prophet, *Call upon me in the day of trouble; I will deliver thee, and thou shalt glorify me.*[1] And again he saith, *It is honourable to reveal and confess the works of God.*[2]

6. Nevertheless, although I am faulty in many things, I wish my brethen and kinsfolk to know what manner of man I am, and that they may be able to understand the desire of my soul.

7. I am not ignorant of *the testimony of* my *Lord,*[3] who witnesseth in the Psalm, *Thou shalt destroy them that speak a lie.*[4] And again he saith, *The mouth that belieth killeth the soul.*[5] And the same Lord saith in the Gospel, *The idle word that men shall speak, they shall give account thereof in the day of judgement.*[6]

8. Wherefore then I ought exceedingly, *with fear and trembling,*[7] to dread this sentence in that day when no one will be able to absent himself or hide, but when all of us, without exception, shall have to *give account* of even the smallest sins *before the judgement seat of* the Lord *Christ.*[8]

9. On this account I had long since thought of writing; but I hesitated until now; for I feared lest I should fall under the censure of men's tongues, and because I have not studied as have others, who in the most approved fashion have drunk in both law and the Holy Scriptures alike, and have never changed their speech from their infancy, but rather have been always rendering it more perfect. For my speech and language is translated into a tongue not my own, as can be easily proved from the savour of my writing, in what fashion I have been taught and am learned in speech; for, saith the wise man, *By the tongue will be discovered understanding and knowledge and the teaching of truth.*[9]

---

[1] Ps. l. 15.   [2] Tob. xii. 7.   [3] 2 Tim. i. 8.
[4] Ps. v. 6.   [5] Wisd. i. 11.   [6] Matt. xii. 36.
[7] Eph. vi. 5.   [8] Rom. xiv. 10, 12.   [9] Ecclus. iv. 29.

10. But what avails an excuse, no matter how true, especially when accompanied by presumption? since now I myself, in mine old age, earnestly desire that which in youth I did not acquire; because my sins prevented me from mastering what I had read through before. But who gives me credence even if I should repeat the statement that I made at the outset?

When a youth, nay, almost a boy, I went into captivity in language [as well as in person] before I knew what I should earnestly desire, or what I ought to shun. And so to-day I blush and am exceedingly afraid to lay bare my lack of education; because I am unable to make my meaning plain in a few words to the learned, for as the Spirit yearns, the [human] disposition displays the souls of men and their understandings.

11. But if I had had [only] the same privileges as others, nevertheless I would not keep silence *on account of the reward* [1] And if perchance it seems to not a few that I am thrusting myself forward in this matter with my want of knowledge and my *slow tongue*, [2] yet it is written, *The tongue of the stammerers shall quickly learn to speak peace.* [3] How much rather should we earnestly desire so to do, who are, he saith, *the epistle of Christ for salvation unto the ends of the earth*, [4] although not a learned one, yet *ministered* most powerfully, *written in your hearts, not with ink, but with the Spirit of the living God.* [5] And again the Spirit witnesseth, *And husbandry* [lit. *rusticity*] *was ordained by the Most High.* [6]

12. Whence I who was at first illiterate, an exile, unlearned verily, who know not how to provide for the future—but this I do know most surely, that *before I was afflicted* [7] I was like a stone lying in the deep mire; and *he that is mighty* [8]

---

[1] Ps. cxix. 112.
[2] Exod iv. 10.
[3] Isa. xxxii. 4.
[4] 2 Cor. iii 2; Acts xiii. 47.
[5] 2 Cor. iii. 3.
[6] Ecclus. vii. 16.
[7] Ps. cxix. 67.
[8] Luke i. 49.

came, and in his mercy lifted me up, and verily raised me
aloft and placed me on the top of the wall. And therefore I
ought to cry aloud that I may also *render somewhat to the
Lord*[1] for his benefits which are so great both here and in
eternity, the value of which the mind of men cannot
estimate.

13. Wherefore then be ye astonied, *ye that fear God, both
small and great,*[2] and ye clever sirs, ye rhetoricians, hear
therefore and search it out. Who was it that called up me,
fool though I be, out of the midst of those who seem to be
wise and skilled in the law, and *powerful in word*[3] and in
everything? And me, moreover, the abhorred of this world,
did he inspire beyond others—if such I were—only that
with reverence and godly fear[4] and *unblameably*[5] I should
faithfully be of service to the nation to whom the love of
Christ conveyed me, and presented me, as long as I live, if
I should be worthy; in fine, that I should with humility
and in truth diligently do them service.

14. And so it is proper that according to *the rule of faith*[6]
in the Trinity, I should define doctrine, and make known
the gift of God and *everlasting consolation,*[7] *without being
held back*[8] by danger, and spread everywhere the name of
God without fear, confidently; so that even *after my decease*[9]
I may leave a legacy to my brethren and sons whom I
baptized in the Lord, many thousands of persons.

15. And I was not worthy, nor such an one, as that the
Lord should grant this to his poor servant, after calamities
and such great difficulties, after a life of slavery, after many
years; that he should bestow on me so great grace towards
that nation, a thing that formerly, in my youth, I never
hoped for nor thought of.

16. Now, after I came to Ireland, tending flocks was my

[1] Ps. cxvi. 12.	[2] Rev. xix. 5.	[3] Acts vii. 22.
[4] Heb. xii. 28.	[5] 1 Thess. ii. 10.	[6] Rom. xii. 3.
[7] 2 Thess. ii. 16.	[8] Phil. ii. 15.	[9] 2 Pet. i. 15.

daily occupation; and constantly I used to pray in the day time. Love of God and the fear of him increased more and more, and faith grew, and the spirit was moved, so that in one day [I would say] as many as a hundred prayers, and at night nearly as many, so that I used to stay even in the woods and on the mountain [to this end]. And before daybreak I used to be roused to prayer, in snow, in frost, in rain; and I felt no hurt; nor was there any sluggishness in me—as I now see, because then *the spirit was fervent*[1] within me.

17. And there verily one night I heard in my sleep a voice saying to me, "Thou fastest to good purpose, thou who art soon to go to thy fatherland." And again, after a very short time, I heard the answer [of God] saying to me, "Lo, thy ship is ready." And it was not near at hand, but was distant perhaps two hundred miles. And I had never been there, nor did I know any one there. And thereupon I shortly took to flight, and left the man with whom I had been for six years, and I came in the strength of God who prospered my way for good, and I met with nothing to alarm me until I reached that ship.

18. And on the very day that I arrived, the ship left its moorings, and I said that I had to [*or* must] sail thence with them; but the shipmaster was annoyed, and replied roughly and angrily, "On no account seek to go with us."

When I heard this, I parted from them to go to the hut where I was lodging, and on the way I began to pray, and before I had finished my prayer, I heard one of them shouting loudly after me, "Come quickly, for these men are calling thee;" and straightway I returned to them.

And they began to say to me, "Come, for we receive thee in good faith; make friends with us in any way thou desirest." And so on that day I refused to be intimate with them [*lit.* suck their breasts], because of the fear of

[1] Acts xviii. 25.

God ; but nevertheless I hoped that some of them would
come into the faith of Jesus Christ, for they were heathen ;
and on this account I continued with them : and forthwith
we set sail.

19. And after three days we reached land, and journeyed
for twenty-eight days through a desert ; and food failed
them, and hunger overcame them. And one day the
shipmaster began to say to me, "How is this, O Christian ?
thou sayest that thy God is great and almighty ; wherefore
then canst thou not pray for us, for we are in danger of
starvation ? Hardly shall we ever see a human being
again."

Then said I plainly to them, "*Turn* in good faith and
with all your heart to [1] the Lord my God, to whom nothing
is impossible, that this day he may send you food in your
journey until ye be satisfied, for he has abundance everywhere."

And, by the help of God, so it came to pass. Lo, a
herd of swine appeared in the way before our eyes, and
they killed many of them ; and in that place they remained
two nights ; and they were well refreshed, and their dogs
were sated, for many of them had fainted and were *left half
dead* [2] by the way.

And after this they rendered hearty thanks to God,
and I became honourable in their eyes ; and from that day
on they had food in abundance. Moreover, they found
wild honey, and *gave* me *a piece of it.* [3] And one of them
said, "*This is offered in sacrifice.*" [4] Thanks be to God,
I tasted none of it.

20. Now on that same night, when I was sleeping, Satan
assailed me mightily, in such sort as I shall remember *as
long as I am in this body.* [5] And he fell upon me as it were
a huge rock, and I had no power over my limbs. But

---

[1] Joel ii. 12.   [2] Luke x. 30.   [3] Luke xxiv. 42.
[4] 1 Cor. x. 28.   [5] 2 Pet i. 13.

whence did it occur to me—to my ignorant mind—to call upon Helias? And on this I saw the sun rise in the heaven, and while I was shouting "Helias" with all my might, lo, the splendour of that sun fell upon me, and straightway shook all weight from off me. And I believe that I was helped by Christ my Lord, and that his Spirit was even then calling aloud on my behalf. And I trust that it will be so *in the day of* my *trouble,*[1] as he saith in the Gospel, *In that day*, the Lord testifieth, *it is not ye that speak, but the Spirit of your Father which speaketh in you.*[2]

21. And, again, after many years, I went into captivity once more. And so on that first night I remained with them. Now I heard the answer of God saying to me, "For two months thou shalt be with them." And so it came to pass. On the sixtieth night after, the Lord delivered me out of their hands.

22. Moreover, he provided for us on our journey food and fire and dry quarters every day, until on the fourteenth day we reached human habitations. As I stated above, for twenty-eight days we journeyed through a desert; and on the night on which we reached human habitations, we had in truth no food left.

23. And again, after a few years, I was in Britain with my kindred, who received me as a son, and in good faith besought me that at all events now, after the great tribulations which I had undergone, I would not depart from them anywhither.

And there verily *I saw in the night visions*[3] a man whose name was Victoricus coming as it were from Ireland with countless letters. And he gave me one of them, and I read the beginning of the letter, which was entitled, "The Voice of the Irish"; and while I was reading aloud the beginning of the letter, I thought that at that very moment I heard the voice of them who lived beside the Wood of

[1] Ps. l. 15.   [2] Matt. x. 20   [3] Dan. vii. 13.

Foclut which is nigh unto the western sea. And thus they cried, as with one mouth, "We beseech thee, holy youth, to come and walk among us once more"

And I was exceedingly *broken in heart*,[1] and could read no further. And so I awoke. Thanks be to God, that after very many years the Lord granted to them according to their cry.

24. And another night, whether within me or beside me, *I cannot tell, God knoweth*,[2] in most admirable words which I heard and could not understand, except that at the end of the prayer he thus affirmed, " He who *laid down his life for thee*,[3] he it is who speaketh in thee." And so I awoke, rejoicing.

25. And another time I saw him praying within me, and I was as it were within my body; and I heard [One praying] over me, that is, over *the inner man* ;[4] and there he was praying mightily with groanings. And meanwhile I was astonied, and was marvelling and thinking who it could be that was praying within me; but at the end of the prayer he affirmed that he was the Spirit. And so I awoke, and I remembered how the Apostle saith, *The Spirit helpeth the infirmities of our prayer, for we know not what we should pray for as we ought ; but the Spirit himself maketh intercession for us with groanings which cannot be uttered, which cannot be expressed in words.*[5] And again, *The Lord our Advocate*[6] *maketh intercession for us* [7]

26. And when I was assailed by not a few of my elders, who came and [urged] my sins against my laborious epis-copate—certainly on that day *I was sore thrust at that I might fall*[8] both here and in eternity. But the Lord graciously spared the stranger and sojourner for his name's sake; and he helped me exceedingly when I was thus

---

[1] Ps. cix. 16. [2] 2 Cor. xii 2.
[3] John x. 11. [4] Eph. iii. 16. [5] Rom. viii. 26.
[6] 1 John ii. 1. [7] Rom. viii. 34. [8] Ps. cxviii. 13.

trampled on, so that I did not come badly into disgrace and reproach. I pray God *that it may not be laid to their charge*[1] as sin.

27. After the lapse of thirty years *they found*, as an *occasion*[2] against me, a matter which I had confessed before I was a deacon. Because of anxiety, with sorrowful mind, I disclosed to my dearest friend things that I had done in my youth one day, nay, in one hour, because I had not yet overcome. *I cannot tell, God knoweth*,[3] if I was then fifteen years old; and I did not believe in the living God, nor had I since my infancy; but I remained in death and in unbelief until I had been chastened exceedingly, and humbled in truth by hunger and nakedness, and that daily.

28. Contrariwise, I did not proceed to Ireland of my own accord until I was nearly worn out. But this was rather well for me, because thus I was amended by the Lord. And he fitted me, so that I should to-day be something which was once far from me, that I should care for, and be busy about, the salvation of others, whereas then I did not even think about myself.

29. And so on that day on which I was *rejected*[4] by the aforesaid persons whom I have mentioned, in that night *I saw in the night visions:*[5]—There was a writing void of honour over against my face. And meanwhile I heard the answer of God saying to me, "We have seen with anger the face of the person designated (the name being expressed)." Nor did he say thus, "Thou hast seen with anger," but, "We have seen with anger," as if in that matter he had joined himself [with me]. As he said, *He that toucheth you is as he that toucheth the apple of mine eye.*[6]

30. Therefore *I thank him who hath enabled me*[7] in all things, because he did not hinder me from the journey on

---

[1] 2 Tim. iv. 16. [2] Dan. vi. 5. [3] 2 Cor. xii. 2.
[4] Ps. cxviii. 22. [5] Dan. vii. 13
[6] Zech. ii. 8 [7] 1 Tim. i. 12.

which I had resolved, and from my labour which I had learnt from Christ my Lord; but rather *I felt in myself* no little *virtue proceeding from him,*[1] and my *faith has been approved*[2] *in the sight of God and of men.*[3]

31. Wherefore then *I say boldly*[4] that my conscience does not blame me either here or hereafter. God is my witness that I have not lied in the matters that I have stated to you.

32. But rather I am grieved for my dearest friend that we should have merited to hear such an answer as that; a man to whom I had even entrusted my soul! And I ascertained from not a few of the brethren before that contention—it was at a time when I was not present, nor was I in Britain, nor will the story originate with me—that he too had fought for me in my absence. Even he himself had said to me with his own lips, "Lo, thou art to be raised to the rank of bishop;" of which I was not worthy. But how did it occur to him afterwards to put me to shame publicly before every one, good and bad, in respect of an [office] which before that he had of his own accord and gladly conceded [to me], and the Lord too, who is *greater than all?*[5]

33. I have said enough. Nevertheless I ought not to hide the gift of God which he bestowed upon us in the land of my captivity; because then I earnestly sought him, and there I found him, and he kept me from all iniquities—this is my belief—*because of his indwelling Spirit*[6] who hath worked in me until this day. Boldly again [am I speaking]. But God knoweth if man had said this to me—perchance I would have held my peace for the love of Christ.

34. Hence therefore I render unwearied thanks to my

---

[1] Mark v. 29, 30. [2] 1 Pet. i. 7. [3] 2 Cor. viii. 21.
[4] Acts ii. 29. [5] John x. 29. [6] Rom. viii. 11.

God who kept me faithful *in the day of* my *temptation,*[1] so that to-day I can confidently offer to him a sacrifice, as *a living victim,*[2] my soul to Christ my Lord who *saved me out of all my troubles,*[3] so that I may say, *Who am I, O Lord,*[4] or what is my calling, that thou hast worked together with me with such divine power? so that to-day among the heathen I should steadfastly exult, and magnify thy name wherever I may be; and that not only in prosperity, but also in troubles, so that whatever may happen to me, whether good or bad, I ought to receive it with an equal mind, and ever render thanks to God who shewed me that I might trust him endlessly, as one that cannot be doubted; and who heard me, so that I, ignorant as I am, and *in the last days,*[5] should be bold to undertake this work so holy and so wonderful; so that I might imitate in some degree those of whom the Lord long ago foretold, when foreshewing that his *Gospel would be for a witness unto all nations* before *the end*[6] of the world. And accordingly, as we see, this has been so fulfilled. Behold, we are witnesses that the Gospel has been preached to the limit beyond which no man dwells.

35. Now it were a tedious task to *declare particularly*[7] the whole of my toil, or even partially [*or*, and in all its parts]. I shall briefly say in what manner the most righteous God often delivered me from slavery and from twelve perils whereby my soul was endangered, besides many plots and *things which I am not able to express in words.*[8] Nor shall I weary my readers But I have as my voucher God who knoweth all things even before they come to pass, as the answer of God frequently warned me, the poor, unlearned orphan.

36. Whence came to me this wisdom, which was not in

---

[1] Ps. xcv. 8. [2] Rom xii. 1. [3] Ps. xxxiv. 6.
[4] 2 Sam. vii. 18. [5] Acts ii. 17. [6] Matt. xxiv. 14
[7] Acts xxi. 19. [8] Rom. viii. 26.

me, I who neither *knew the number of my days,*[1] nor cared for God ? Whence afterwards came to me that gift so great, so salutary, the knowledge and love of God, but only that I might part with fatherland and kindred ?

37. And many gifts were proffered me with weeping and tears. And I displeased them, and also, against my wish, not a few of my elders ; but, God being my guide, in no way did I consent or yield to them. It was not any grace in me, but God who overcometh in me ; and he withstood them all, so that I came to the heathen Irish to preach the Gospel, and to endure insults from unbelievers, so as to *hear the reproach of my going abroad,*[2] and [endure] many persecutions *even unto bonds,*[3] and that I should give up my free condition for the profit of others. And if I should be worthy, I am ready [to give] even *my* life *for his name's sake*[4] unhesitatingly and very gladly ; and there I desire to spend it even unto death, if the Lord would grant it to me.

38. Because I am a debtor exceedingly to God, who granted me such great grace that many peoples through me should be regenerated to God and afterwards confirmed, and that clergy should everywhere be ordained for them for a people newly come to belief, which the Lord took *from the ends of the earth,* as he had in times past promised through his prophets : *The Gentiles shall come unto thee from the ends of the earth, and shall say, As our fathers have got for themselves false idols, and there is no profit in them.*[5] And again, *I have set thee to be a light of the Gentiles, that thou shouldest be for salvation unto the ends of the earth.*[6]

39. And there I wish to *wait for his promise*[7] who verily never disappoints. As he promises in the Gospel, *They shall come from the east and west and from the south and from the north, and shall sit down with Abraham and Isaac*

---

[1] Ps. xxxix. 4.   [2] Ecclus. xxix. 29.   [3] 2 Tim. ii. 9.
[4] 3 John 7.   [5] Jer. xvi. 19.
[6] Acts xiii. 47.   [7] Acts i. 4.

D

and Jacob;[1] as we believe that believers will come from all parts of the world.

40. For that reason therefore, we ought to fish well and diligently, as the Lord forewarns and teaches, saying, *Come ye after me, and I will make you to become fishers of men.*[2] And again he saith through the prophets, *Behold I send fishers and many hunters, saith God,*[3] and so forth.

Wherefore then, it was exceedingly necessary that we should spread our nets so that a *great multitude*[4] and a throng should be taken for God, and that everywhere there should be clergy to baptize and exhort a people poor and needy, as the Lord in the Gospel warns and teaches, saying, *Go ye therefore now and teach all nations, baptizing them in the name of the Father, and of the Son, and of the Holy Ghost: teaching them to observe all things whatsoever I have commanded you: and, lo, I am with you alway, even unto the end of the world.*[5] And again he saith, *Go ye therefore into all the world, and preach the Gospel to every creature. He that believeth and is baptized shall be saved; but he that believeth not shall be damned.*[6] And again, *This Gospel of the kingdom shall be preached in all the world for a witness unto all nations: and then shall the end come.*[7]

And in like manner the Lord, foreshewing by the prophet, saith, *And it shall come to pass in the last days, saith the Lord, I will pour out of my Spirit upon all flesh: and your sons and your daughters shall prophesy, and your young men shall see visions, and your old men shall dream dreams: and on my servants and on my handmaidens I will pour out in those days of my Spirit; and they shall prophesy.*[8] And Hosea saith, *I will call them my people, which were not my people; and her one that hath obtained mercy which had not obtained mercy. And it shall come to pass, that in the place*

---

[1] Matt. viii. 11.
[2] Matt. iv. 19.
[3] Jer. xvi. 16
[4] Luke v. 6.
[5] Matt. xxviii. 19, 20.
[6] Mark xvi. 15, 16.
[7] Matt. xxiv. 14.
[8] Acts ii. 17, 18.

where it was said, Ye are not my people; there shall they be called the children of the living God.[1]

41. Wherefore then in Ireland they who never had the knowledge of God, but until now only worshipped idols and abominations—how has there been lately *prepared a people*[2] of the Lord, and they are called children of God? Sons and daughters of Scottic chieftains are seen to become monks and virgins of Christ.

42. In especial there was one blessed lady of Scottic birth, of noble rank, most beautiful, grown up, whom I baptized; and after a few days she came to us for a certain cause. She disclosed to us that she had been warned by an angel of God, and that he counselled her to become a virgin of Christ, and live closer to God. Thanks be to God, six days after, most admirably and eagerly she seized on that which all virgins of God do in like manner; not with the consent of their fathers; but they endure persecution and lying reproaches from their kindred; and nevertheless their number increases more and more—and as for those of our race who are born there, we know not the number of them—besides widows and continent persons.

But the women who are kept in slavery suffer especially; they constantly endure even unto terrors and threats. But the Lord gave grace to many of his handmaidens, for although they are forbidden, they earnestly follow the example [set them].

43. Wherefore then, even if I should wish to part with them, and thus proceeding to Britain—and glad and ready I was to do so—as to my fatherland and kindred, and not that only, but to go as far as Gaul in order to visit the brethren and to behold the face of the saints of my Lord—God knoweth that I used to desire it exceedingly—yet *I am bound in the Spirit, who witnesseth to me*[3] that if I should do this, he would note me as guilty; and I fear to lose the

---

[1] Rom. ix. 25, 26.   [2] Luke i. 17.   [3] Acts xx. 22, 23.

labour which I began; and yet not I, but Christ the Lord who commanded me to come and be with them for the remainder of my life, if the Lord will, and if he should keep me from every evil way, so that I may not sin in his sight.

44. Now I hope that I ought to do this; but I do not trust myself *as long as I am in the body of this death*,[1] because he is strong who daily endeavours to turn me away from the faith, and from that chastity of unfeigned religion which I have purposed to keep to the end of my life for Christ my Lord.   But the flesh, the enemy, is ever dragging us unto death, that is, to enticements to do that which is forbidden.   And *I know in part*[2] wherein I have not led a perfect life as have other believers, but I confess to my Lord, and I do not blush in his presence, for I lie not:—From the time that I knew him, from my youth, there grew in me the love of God and the fear of him; and unto this hour, the Lord being gracious to me, *I have kept the faith*.[3]

45. Let who will laugh and insult, I shall not be silent nor conceal the signs and wonders which were shewn to me by the Lord many years before they came to pass; since he knoweth all things even *before the world began*.[4]

46. Wherefore then I ought without ceasing to render thanks to God who oftentimes pardoned my folly and carelessness—and that not in one place only—so that he be not exceedingly wroth with me, to whom I have been given as a fellow-labourer; and yet I did not quickly yield in accordance with what had been shewn to me, and as *the Spirit brought to my remembrance*[5] And the Lord *shewed mercy upon me thousands of times*,[6] because he saw in me that I was ready, but that I did not know through these [revelations] what I should do about my position,

---

[1] 2 Pet. i. 13; Rom. vii. 24.   [2] 1 Cor. xiii. 9.   [3] 2 Tim. iv. 7.
[4] 2 Tim. i. 9.   [5] John xiv. 26.   [6] Exod. xx. 6.

because many were forbidding this embassage. Moreover they used to talk amongst themselves behind my back and say, "Why does this fellow thrust himself into danger amongst hostile people *who know not God?*"[1] They did not say this out of malice; but it did not seem meet in their eyes, on account of my illiteracy, as I myself witness that I have understood. And I did not quickly recognize the grace that was then in me. Now that seems meet in mine eyes which I ought to have done before.

47. Now therefore, I have frankly disclosed to my brethren and fellow-servants who have believed me, for what reason *I told you before, and foretell you*[2] to strengthen and confirm your faith. Would that you, too, would imitate greater things, and do things of more consequence! This will be my glory, for *a wise son is the glory of his father.*[3]

48. You know, and God also, in what manner I have lived from my youth with you, in the faith of truth and in sincerity of heart. Moreover, as regards those heathen amongst whom I dwell, I have kept faith with them, and will keep it. God knoweth I have *defrauded none*[4] of them, nor do I think of doing it, for the sake of God and his Church, lest I should raise persecution against them and all of us, and lest through me the name of the Lord should be blasphemed; for it is written, *Woe to the man through whom the name of the Lord is blasphemed.*[5]

49. *But though I be rude in all things,*[6] nevertheless I have endeavoured in some sort to keep myself, both for the Christian brethren, and the virgins of Christ, and the *devout women*[7] who used of their own accord to present me with their little gifts, and would cast of their ornaments upon the altar; and I returned them again to them. And they were scandalized at my doing so. But I did it on account

[1] 2 Thess i 8. [2] 2 Cor. xiii. 2. [3] Prov. x. 1.
[4] 2 Cor. vii. 2. [5] Matt. xviii. 7; Rom. ii. 24. [6] 2 Cor. xi 6.
[7] Acts xiii. 50.

of the hope of immortality, so as to keep myself warily in all things; for this reason, namely, that the heathen might receive me and the ministry of my service on any grounds, and that I should not, even in the smallest matter, give occasion to the unbelievers to defame or disparage.

50. Perchance then, when I baptized so many thousands of men, I hoped from any one of them even as much as the half of a scruple. *Tell me and I shall restore it to you.*[1] Or when the Lord ordained clergy everywhere by means of my mediocrity, and I imparted my service to them for nothing, if I demanded from one of them even the price of my *shoe; tell it against me and I shall restore you*[1] more.

51. *I spent for you*[2] that they might receive me; and both amongst you and wherever I journeyed for your sake, through many perils, even to outlying regions beyond which no man dwelt, and where never had any one come to baptize, or ordain clergy, or confirm the people, I have, by the bounty of the Lord, initiated everything, carefully and very gladly, for your salvation.

52. On occasion, I used to give presents to the kings, besides the hire that I gave to their sons who accompany me; and nevertheless they seized me with my companions. And on that day they most eagerly desired to kill me; but my time had not yet come. And everything they found with us they plundered, and me myself they bound with irons. And on the fourteenth day the Lord delivered me from their power; and whatever was ours was restored to us for the sake of God and the *near friends*[3] whom we had provided beforehand.

53. Moreover, ye know by proof how much I paid to those who were judges throughout all the districts which I more frequently visited; for I reckon that I distributed to them not less than the price of fifteen men, so that ye might enjoy me, and I might ever enjoy you in God. I

---

[1] 1 Sam. xii. 3.   [2] 2 Cor. xii. 15.   [3] Acts x. 24.

do not regret it, nor is it enough for me. Still *I spend and will spend more.*[1] The Lord is mighty to grant to me afterwards to be myself *spent for your souls.*[1]

54. Behold, *I call God for a record upon my soul*[2] *that I lie not;*[3] nor would I write to you that there may be *an occasion for flattering words or covetousness,*[4] nor that I hope for honour from any of you. Sufficient to me is the honour which is not seen as yet, but is believed on in the heart. And *faithful is he that promised;*[5] never does he lie.

55. But I see that already *in this present world*[6] I am exalted above measure by the Lord. And I was not worthy nor such a one as that he should grant this to me; since I know most surely that poverty and affliction become me better than delights and riches. But Christ the Lord, too, was poor for our sakes. I indeed am wretched and unfortunate; and though I should wish for wealth, now I have it not; *nor do I judge mine own self;*[7] for daily I expect either slaughter, or to be defrauded, or reduced to slavery, or an unfair attack of some kind. *But none of these things move me,*[8] on account of the promises of heaven, because I have cast myself into the hands of God Almighty, for he rules everywhere, as saith the prophet, *Cast thy care upon God, and he shall sustain thee.*[9]

56. Behold now *I commit the keeping of my soul to my most faithful*[10] God, *for whom I am an ambassador*[11] in my ignoble state, only because he accepteth no man's person, and chose me for this duty that I should be one of his least ministers.

57. Wherefore then, *I shall render unto him for all his benefits*[12] towards me. But what shall I say, or what shall I promise to my Lord? For I am only worth what he him-

[1] 2 Cor. xii. 15   [2] 2 Cor. i. 23   [3] Gal. i 20.
[4] 1 Thess ii 5.   [5] Heb. x. 23.   [6] Gal. i 4.
[7] 1 Cor. iv 3.   [8] Acts xx. 24   [9] Ps lv. 22.
[10] 1 Pet. iv. 19.   [11] Eph. vi. 20.   [12] Ps. cxvi. 12

self has given to me. But *he trieth the hearts and reins,*[1] [and knoweth] that enough, and more than enough, do I desire, and was ready, that he should grant me to *drink of his cup,*[2] as he granted to others also who love him.

58. On which account let it not happen to me from my God that I should ever part with his *people which he purchased*[3] in the ends of the earth. I pray God to give me perseverance, and to vouchsafe that I bear to him faithful witness, until my passing hence, for the sake of my God.

59. And if I ever imitated anything good for the sake of my God whom I love, I pray him to grant to me that I may shed my blood with those strangers and captives for his name's sake, even though I should lack burial itself, or that in most wretched fashion my corpse be divided limb by limb to dogs and wild beasts, or that the fowls of the air eat it. Most surely I deem that if this should happen to me, I have gained my soul as well as my body, because without any doubt we shall rise on that day in the clear shining of the sun, that is, in the glory of Christ Jesus our Redeemer, as *sons of the living God*[4] and *joint heirs with Christ,*[5] and *conformed to his image*[6] that will be; since *of him and through him and in him*[7] we shall reign.

60. For that sun which we behold, by the command of God rises daily for our sakes; but it will never reign, nor will its splendour endure; but all those who worship it shall—wretched men—come badly to punishment. We, on the other hand, who believe in and worship the true sun, Christ—who will never perish, nor will any one *who doeth his will;*[8] but he *will abide for ever,* as Christ *will abide for ever,*[9] who reigneth with God the Father Almighty and with the Holy Spirit, before the worlds, and now, and for ever and ever. Amen.

[1] Ps. vii. 9.   [2] Matt. xx. 22.   [3] Isa. xliii. 21.
[4] Rom. ix. 26.   [5] Rom. viii. 17.   [6] Rom. viii. 29
[7] Rom. xi. 36.   [8] 1 John ii. 17.   [9] Ps. lxxxix. 36.

61. Lo, again and again I shall briefly set forth the words of my confession: *I testify* in truth and in exultation of heart *before God and his holy angels*,[1] that I never had any cause except the Gospel and his promises for ever returning to that nation from whence previously I scarcely escaped.

62. But I pray those who believe in and fear God, whosoever shall have vouchsafed to look upon and receive this writing which Patrick the sinner, unlearned verily, composed in Ireland, that no one ever say it was my ignorance that did whatever trifling matter I did, or proved, in accordance with God's good pleasure; but judge ye, and let it be most truly believed that it was the gift of God. And this is my confession before I die.

[1] I Tim. v. 21.

INTRODUCTION TO THE LETTER

EVER since the days of Ussher and Ware, this document has been usually known as the *Epistola ad Coroticum;* but St. Patrick himself describes it (c. 2) as "sent to the soldiers of Coroticus," a considerable number of whom were Christians by profession. It is a-manifesto, a protest, which its author hoped would be read in the presence of Coroticus himself (c. 21).

It was called forth by the failure of a previous letter and a deputation of clerics to touch the hearts of the British raiders (c. 3). Muirchu (i. 29) says, "Patrick . . . endeavoured by a letter to recall him [Coroticus] to the way of truth, but he mocked at his salutary warnings." This reference is, in all likelihood, a characteristically muddle-headed confusion of the extant letter with that to which Patrick refers in c. 3. On the other hand, the language of Muirchu is consistent with the supposition that he had not read the document in our hands; though I think he had.

As to Coroticus himself, it is now quite certain that he is not to be identified with the Caredig who gave his name to the county of Cardigan (so Todd; *St. Patrick,* p. 352), but with Ceretic who ruled under the Romans in Strathclyde about A.D. 420–450, or later. This identification, first suggested by Sir Samuel Ferguson (*Patrician Documents,* xxxii.), has been proved conclusively by Prof. Zimmer (*Celtic Church,* pp. 54, 55). Prof. Bury conjectures that the date of the raid of Coroticus was 459. His capital was Alcluith (the Rock of Clyde, Dumbarton). He is called the " King

of Ail" in the title of c. 29 of Muirchu's Life, Book i.
("Regem Aloo," *Aloo* is genitive of *Ail*). Ail is evidently
Alcluith (see the authorities cited by Prof. Bury, *St. Patrick*,
p. 314). Prof. Bury remarks that "this identification agrees
with the close association of Patrick's Coroticus with the
Picts and Scots, which shews that he must have ruled
in Northern Britain."

THE LETTER

1. Patrick the sinner, unlearned verily:—I confess that I am a bishop, appointed by God, in Ireland. Most surely I deem that from God I have received what I am. And so I dwell in the midst of barbarians, a stranger and an exile for the love of God. He is witness if this is so. Not that I desired to utter from my mouth anything so harshly and so roughly; but I am compelled *by zeal for God*;[1] and *the truth of Christ*[2] roused me, for the love of my nearest friends and sons, for whom I have *not regarded* my fatherland and kindred, yea nor my *life, even unto death*,[3] if I am worthy. I have vowed to my God to teach the heathen, though I be despised by some.

2. With mine own hand have I written and composed these words to be given and delivered and sent to the soldiers of Coroticus—I do not say to my fellow-citizens or to the fellow-citizens of the holy Romans, but to those who are fellow-citizens of demons because of their evil deeds. Behaving like enemies, they are dead while they live, allies of the Scots and apostate Picts, as though wishing to gorge themselves with blood, the blood of innocent Christians, whom I in countless numbers begot to God and confirmed in Christ.

3. On the day following that on which the newly baptized, in white array, were anointed—it was still fragrant on their foreheads while they were cruelly butchered and slaughtered with the sword by the aforesaid

---

[1] Rom. x. 2.   [2] 2 Cor. xi. 10.   [3] Phil. ii. 30.

persons—I sent a letter with a holy presbyter whom I had taught from his infancy, clergy accompanying him, with a request that they would grant us some of the booty and of the baptized captives whom they had taken. They jeered at them.

4. Therefore I know not what I should the rather mourn: whether those who are slain, or those whom they captured, or those whom the devil grievously ensnared. In everlasting punishment they will become slaves of hell along with him; for verily *whosoever committeth sin is a bondservant of sin,*[1] and is called *a son of the devil.*[2]

5. On this account let every man that feareth God learn that aliens they are from me and from Christ my God, *for whom I am an ambassador*[3]—patricide, fratricide as he is!— *ravening wolves*[4] *eating up the people* of the Lord *as it were bread.*[5] As he saith, *O Lord, the ungodly have destroyed thy law,*[6] which in the last times he had excellently [and] kindly planted in Ireland; and it was builded by the favour of God.

6. I make no false claim. I have part with those whom *he called and predestinated*[7] to preach the Gospel amidst no small persecutions, *even unto the ends of the earth,*[8] even though the enemy casts an evil eye on me by means of the tyranny of Coroticus, who fears neither God nor his priests whom he chose, and to whom he granted that highest, divine, sublime power, that *whom they should bind on earth should be bound in heaven.*[9]

7. Whence therefore, *ye holy and humble men of heart,*[10] I beseech you very much. It is not right to pay court to such men, nor to take food or drink with them; nor ought one to accept their almsgivings, until [doing] sore penance

---

[1] John viii. 34. [2] Acts xiii 10. [3] Eph. vi. 20.
[4] Acts xx. 29. [5] Ps. xiv. 4. [6] Ps. cxix. 126.
[7] Rom. viii. 30. [8] Acts xiii. 47.
[9] Matt. xvi. 19. [10] Dan. iii. 87.

with shedding of tears, they make amends to God, and liberate the servants of God and the baptized handmaidens of Christ, for whom he died and was crucified.

8. *The most High approveth not the gifts of the wicked. He that offereth sacrifice of the goods of the poor is as one that sacrificeth the son in the presence of his father.*[1] The riches, he saith, *which he hath gathered unjustly will be vomited up from his belly. The angel of death draggeth him away. He will be tormented by the fury of dragons. The viper's tongue shall slay him; unquenchable fire devoureth him.*[2]

And therefore, *Woe to those who fill themselves with what is not their own.*[3] And, *What is a man profited, if he shall gain the whole world, and lose his own soul?*[4]

9. It would be tedious to discuss or declare [their deeds] one by one, [and] to gather from the whole law testimonies concerning such greed. Avarice is a deadly sin; *Thou shalt not covet thy neighbour's goods; Thou shalt do no murder;*[5] *A murderer cannot be with Christ; He that hateth his brother is reckoned as a murderer.* And again, *He that loveth not his brother abideth in death.*[6] How much more guilty is he that hath stained his hands with the blood of the sons of God whom he recently purchased in the ends of the earth through the exhortation of our littleness.

10. Was it without God, or according to the flesh, that I came to Ireland? Who compelled me? *I am bound in the Spirit*[7] not to see any one of my kinsfolk. Is it from me that springs that godly compassion which I exercise towards that nation who once took me captive, and made havoc of the menservants and maidservants of my father's house? I was freeborn according to the flesh; I am born of a father who was a decurion; but I sold my noble rank

---

[1] Ecclus. xxxiv. 23, 24.   [2] Job xx. 15, 16.
[3] Hab. ii. 6.   [4] Matt. xvi. 26.
[5] Rom. xiii. 9.   [6] 1 John iii. 14, 15.   [7] Acts. xx. 22.

—I blush not to state it, nor am I sorry—for the profit of others; in short, I am a slave in Christ to a foreign nation for the unspeakable glory of the *eternal life which is in Christ Jesus our Lord.*[1]

11. And if my own know me not, *a prophet hath no honour in his own country.*[2] Perchance we are not of *the one fold,*[3] nor have *one God and Father.*[4] As he saith, *He that is not with me is against me, and he that gathereth not with me scattereth abroad.*[5] It is not meet that *one pulleth down and another buildeth up.*[6] *I seek not mine own.*[7]

It was not any grace in me, but God that *put this earnest care into my heart,*[8] that I should be one of the *hunters* or *fishers*[9] whom long ago God foreshowed would come *in the last days.*[10]

12. Men look askance at me. What shall I do, O Lord? I am exceedingly despised. Lo, around me are thy sheep torn to pieces and spoiled, and that too by the robbers aforesaid, by the orders of Coroticus with hostile disposition.

Far from the love of God is he who betrays Christians into the hands of the Scots and Picts. *Ravening wolves*[11] have swallowed up the flock of the Lord which verily in Ireland was growing up excellently with the greatest care. And the sons and daughters of Scottic chieftains who were monks and virgins of Christ I cannot reckon. Wherefore, *be not pleased with the wrong done to the just; even unto hell it shall not please thee.*[12]

13. Which of the saints would not shudder to jest and feast with such men? They have filled their houses with the spoil of dead Christians. They live by plunder. Wretched men, they know not that it is poison; they offer the deadly food to their friends and sons; just as Eve did

---

[1] Rom. vi. 23. [2] John iv. 44. [3] John x. 16.
[4] Eph. iv. 6; Mal ii. 10. [5] Matt. xii. 30. [6] Ecclus. xxxiv. 28.
[7] I Cor. xiii. 5. [8] 2 Cor. viii. 16. [9] Jer. xvi. 16.
[10] Acts ii. 17. [11] Acts xx. 29. [12] Ecclus. ix. 17.

not understand that verily it was death that she handed to her husband. So are all they who do wrong; they work death as their eternal punishment.

14. This is the custom of the Roman Gauls:—They send holy and fit men to the Franks and other heathen with many thousands of *solidi* to redeem baptized captives. Thou rather slayest and sellest them to a foreign *nation which knows not God.*[1] Thou handest over *the members of Christ*[2] as it were to a brothel. What manner of hope in God hast thou, or has he who consents with thee, or who holds converse with thee in words of flattery? God will judge; for it is written, *Not only those who commit evil, but those that consent with them shall be damned.*[3]

15. I know not *what I should say, or what I should speak*[4] further about the departed ones of the sons of God, whom the sword has touched roughly above measure. For it is written, *Weep with them that weep,*[5] and again, *If one member suffer, let all the members suffer with it.*[6] On this account the Church bewails and laments her sons and daughters whom the sword has not as yet slain, but who are banished and carried off to distant lands where sin openly, grievously, and shamelessly abounds. There freemen are put up for sale, Christians are reduced to slavery, and, worst of all, to most degraded, most vile and apostate Picts.

16. Therefore in sadness and grief shall I cry aloud: O most lovely and beloved brethen, and sons whom *I begot in Christ*[7]—I cannot reckon them—what shall I do for you? I am not worthy to come to the aid of either God or men. *The wickedness of the wicked hath prevailed against us.*[8] *We are become* as it were *strangers.*[9] Perchance they do not believe that we receive *one baptism,* and that we have *one God and Father.*[10] It is in their eyes a disgraceful thing that

---

[1] I Thess. iv. 5.   [2] I Cor. vi. 15.   [3] Rom. i. 32.
[4] John xii. 49.   [5] Rom. xii. 15.   [6] I Cor. xii. 26.
[7] I Cor. iv. 15.   [8] Ps. lxv. 3.   [9] Ps. lxix. 8.   [10] Eph. iv. 5.

we were born in Ireland. As he saith, *Have ye not one God? Why do ye, each one, forsake his neighbour?*[1]

17. Therefore, I grieve for you, I grieve, O ye most dear to me. But again, I rejoice within myself. *I have not laboured* for nought, and my going abroad was not *in vain.*[2] And there happened a crime so horrid and unspeakable! Thanks be to God, it was as baptized believers that ye departed from the world to Paradise. I can see you. Ye have begun to remove to where *there shall be no night nor sorrow nor death any more;*[3] but *ye shall leap like calves loosened from their bands, and ye shall tread down the wicked, and they shall be ashes under your feet.*[4]

18. Ye therefore shall reign with apostles and prophets and martyrs. Ye shall take everlasting kingdoms, as he himself witnesseth, saying, *They shall come from the east and west, and shall sit down with Abraham and Isaac and Jacob in the kingdom of heaven.*[5] *Without are dogs and sorcerers and murderers; and liars and false swearers shall have their part in the lake of everlasting fire*[6] Not without just cause the apostle saith, *Where the righteous shall scarcely be saved, where shall the sinner and the ungodly transgressor of the law recognize himself?*[7]

19. Wherefore then, where shall Coroticus with his accursed followers, rebels against Christ, where shall they see themselves?—they who distribute baptized damsels as rewards, and that for the sake of a wretched temporal kingdom, which verily passes away in a moment like a cloud or *smoke which is* verily *dispersed by the wind.*[8] *So shall the* deceitful *wicked perish at the presence of the Lord; but let the righteous feast*[9] in great constancy with Christ *They shall judge nations, and rule*[10] over ungodly kings for ever and ever. Amen.

---

[1] Mal. ii. 10. [2] Phil. ii. 16. [3] Rev. xxii 5; xxi. 4.
[4] Mal. iv. 2, 3. [5] Matt. viii. 11. [6] Rev. xxii. 15; xxi. 8.
[7] 1 Pet. iv. 18. [8] Wisd. v. 15. [9] Ps. lxviii. 2, 3. [10] Wisd. iii. 8

E

20. *I testify before God and his angels*[1] that it will be so, as he has signified to my unskilfulness. The words are not mine, but of God and the apostles and prophets, who have never lied, which I have set forth in Latin. *He that believeth shall be saved, but he that believeth not shall be damned.*[2] God hath spoken.

21. I beseech very much that whatever servant of God be ready, he be the bearer of this letter, that on no account it be suppressed or concealed by any one, but much rather be read in the presence of all the people, yea, in the presence of Coroticus himself; if so be that God may inspire them to amend their lives to God some time; so that even though late they may repent of their impious doings—murderer of the brethren of the Lord!—and may liberate the baptized women captives whom they had taken, so that they may deserve to live to God, and be made whole, both here and in eternity.

Peace—to the Father, and to the Son, and 'to the Holy Ghost. Amen.

---

[1] 1 Tim. v. 21

[2] Mark xvi. 16.

INTRODUCTION TO THE LORICA OF
ST. PATRICK

THE Irish hymn commonly known as "The Lorica of
St. Patrick" is preserved in three ancient MSS.: (1) the
Irish Liber Hymnorum (eleventh century), in the Library
of Trinity College, Dublin; (2) the copy (fourteenth or
fifteenth century) of the Tripartite Life, in the Bodleian
Library, Oxford, and (3) a MS. in the British Museum
(Egerton 93), which is of lesser importance. It was first
published, with a translation by Dr. O'Donovan, in 1839,
by Dr. Petrie, in a paper on the History and Antiquities of
Tara Hill (*Transactions R.I.A.* xviii., p. 56 ff.). The best
critical editions are that of Prof. Atkinson in *The Irish
Liber Hymnorum*, 1898, and that of Dr. Whitley Stokes and
Mr. J. Strachan, in *Thesaurus Palæohibernicus*, 1903.

The translation printed here is that of Dr. Atkinson (A),
with certain corrections suggested by Mr. E. J. Gwynn,
and some important variations noted from the translation
by Stokes and Strachan (S) I have changed A's *might* to
in the might in the stanzas i. 1; ii.; iii. 1; iv. 1; v. 1;
viii. 1. Mr. Gwynn says that *niurt* here is a dative, and
should mean "by (or *in*, or *with*) the might." The rendering of i. 5, "towards the Creator," is that of Miss E. Knott,
approved by Mr. Gwynn. The other places in which Mr
Gwynn's corrections of A will be found are, iii. 2; v. last
line; vi. 6.

A *lorica* (breast-plate, or "religious armour," as Petrie
renders it) is a hymn or rhythmical prayer the recitation
of which was believed to ensure special divine protection.
There are others of the same class of composition extant.
They have been made the subject of special study in

valuable papers by Miss Eleanor Hull ("The Ancient Hymn-charms of Ireland," *Folk-lore*, xxi. 4, 1910) and L Gougaud "Étude sur les *loricæ* Celtiques," *Bulletin d'Ancienne Littérature et d'Archéologie*, 1911, 1912). M Gougaud enumerates two in Latin, eleven in Irish and two in Welsh. The term *lorica* is derived from the phrase of St Paul in Eph vi. 14, *induti loricam iustitiæ* In one or two cases the *breastplate* is the Divine Person invoked; but generally it is the formula itself, an adaptation to Christian use, and in Christian terminology, of the forms of pagan spells. The *Lorica* of St. Patrick is not only the most ancient of those that are extant, but it is also the most spiritual in tone. M Gougaud can find no parallels to stanzas iv. and v. in the other *loricæ* known to him. It is possible, as Miss Hull has suggested to me, that our *Lorica* is "a group of these charm-hymns thrown together either by St. Patrick or some other very early composer, and formed into one very fine hymn" There is a peculiarly Patrician touch in stanza iv., which reminds us of his address to Ethne and Fedelm, p. 132, and the intense personal devotion to Christ expressed in stanza vii has parallels in the Confession.

This *lorica* is undoubtedly very ancient. Stanza vi., in particular, reflects a time when paganism was still formidable But the most convincing proof of its antiquity is the language. The precise meaning of many of the words is still conjectural.

There does not seem to be any reason for denying that St. Patrick composed this hymn. In the Book of Armagh (fol 16 r° *a*) there is a note by the scribe, of "the fourfold honour due to St. Patrick in all the monasteries and churches throughout Ireland." The last item is, "Canticum eius Scotticum semper canere." All that can be inferred from Muirchu's silence on the subject is that he was ignorant of the story as to the occasion of its composition as given in the Tripartite Life and in the Preface quoted below. Prof. Atkinson remarks (*op. cit.* ii. 210), "The language of the hymn is so uncouth in its grammatical forms that it affords no sure basis for argument. But, at least, it is more likely that the grammatical anomalies should be survivals of perversions of some older forms of speech than that they should have been deliberately constructed in times subsequent to St. Patrick to give the piece an archaic flavour."

According to Petrie (*op. cit.* p. 69) the use of the hymn as a *lorica* had not died out in his time (1839). His words are: "It is remarkable that the *Luireach Phadrig* is still remembered popularly in many parts of Ireland, and a portion of it is to this day repeated by the people, usually at bed-time." Miss E. Hull, however, is inclined to think that it is not St. Patrick's *Lorica* that is remembered; but the old charm forms, familiar everywhere in Celtic lands, out of which St. Patrick's *Lorica* grew.

The following is the ancient Irish Preface to the hymn :—

PREFACE TO ST. PATRICK'S LORICA
(Prof. Atkinson's Translation)

PATRICK made this hymn; in the time of Loegaire macNeill it was made, and the cause of its composition was for the protection of himself and his monks against the deadly enemies that lay in ambush for the clerics. And it is a lorica of faith for the protection of body and soul against demons and men and vices: when any person shall recite it daily with pious meditation on God, demons shall not dare to face him, it shall be a protection to him against all poison and envy; it shall be a guard to him against sudden death, it shall be a lorica for his soul after his decease.

Patrick sang it when the ambuscades were laid for him by Loegaire, in order that he should not go to Tara to sow the Faith, so that on that occasion they were seen before those who were lying in ambush as if they were wild deer having behind them a fawn, viz. Benen [Benignus], and "Deer's Cry" [*Faeth Fiada*] is its name.

In the account given by Muirchu (i. 18) of the transformation of St. Patrick and his companions into deer, there is no mention of this hymn. This is not a proof that Muirchu did not know of the hymn as Patrick's; but it does suggest that the association of the name *Faeth Fiada* with the story told by Muirchu is due to a false derivation of the name in later times when the original meaning of it had been lost. Prof. Atkinson (*Liber Hymnorum*, ii. 209) gives reasons which suggest that *Faeth Fiada* is the same as *feth fiadha*, "a spell, peculiar to druids and poets, who by pronouncing certain verses made themselves invisible." In the paper by Miss Eleanor Hull, already referred to, it is shewn that this kind of spell, called *fath fiadhe* in Scottish Gaelic, is still well known in Scotland.

ST. PATRICK'S LORICA

I

I arise to-day :
> in vast might, invocation of the Trinity,
> belief in a Threeness;
> confession of Oneness;
> towards the Creator [A, meeting in the Creator
>   S, of the Creator of Creation].

II

I arise to-day :
> in the might of Christ's Birth and His Baptism;
> in the might of His Crucifixion and Burial;
> in the might of His Resurrection and Ascension;
> in the might of His Descent to the Judgment of Doom.

III

I arise to-day :

    in the might of the order of Cherubim [A, of grades
        of Cherubim ; S, of the love of Cherubim];

    in obedience of Angels ;

    in ministration of Archangels ;

    in hope of resurrection for the sake of reward ;

    in prayers of Patriarchs ;

    in predictions of Prophets ;

    in preachings of Apostles ;

    in faiths of Confessors ;

    in innocence of holy Virgins ;

    in deeds of righteous men.

IV

I arise to-day :

    in the might of Heaven ;

    brightness of Sun ;

    whiteness of Snow [S, brilliance of Moon] ;

    splendour of Fire ;

    speed of Lightning [A, Light] ;

    swiftness of Wind ;

    depth of Sea ;

    stability of Earth ;

    firmness of Rock.

V

I arise to-day :

in the might of God	for my piloting ;
Power of God	for my upholding
Wisdom of God	for my guidance ;
Eye of God	for my foresight ;
Ear of God	for my hearing ;
Word of God	for my utterance ;
Hand of God	for my guardianship ;

Path of God   for my precedence [S, to lie
                        before me] ;
Shield of God   for my protection ;
Host of God   for my salvation ;
    against snares of demons ;
    against allurements of vices ;
    against solicitations of nature ;
    against every person that wishes me ill
    far and near ;
    one or many [A, alone and in a crowd].

VI

I invoke therefore all these forces :
    against [A, to intervene between me and] every fierce
        merciless force that may come upon my body and
        my soul ;
    against incantations of false prophets ;
    against black laws of paganism ;
    against false laws of heresy ;
    against encompassment of idolatry [A, deceit of
        idolatry] ;
    against spells of women and smiths and druids ;
    against all knowledge that is forbidden the human
        soul.

VII

Christ for my guardianship to-day :
    against poison, against burning,
    against drowning, against wounding,
  that there may come to me a multitude of rewards ;
Christ with me, Christ before me,
Christ behind me, Christ in me,
Christ under me, Christ over me,
Christ to right of me, Christ to left of me,

Christ in lying down, Christ in sitting, Christ in rising up,
Christ in the heart of every person, who may think of me!
Christ in the mouth of every one, who may speak to me!
Christ in every eye, which may look on me!
Christ in every ear, which may hear me!

I arise to-day:

> in vast might, invocation of the Trinity
> belief in a Threeness;
> confession of Oneness;
> meeting in the Creator;

Domini est salus, Domini est salus, Christi est salus;
Salus tua, Domine, sit semper nobiscum.

SAYINGS OF PATRICK

In the Book of Armagh, at the foot of fol. 9, r° *a*, are
written three disjointed sentences with the title *Dicta
Patricii.* The second of these Sayings is a citation from
Letter, 17. For the first and third, see Introduction, pp.
11 and 15 f. respectively. For St. Patrick's use of *Deo
gratias* see note on Conf. 19 There is a critical examination of the *Dicta Patricii* in Bury's *St. Patrick*, p. 228 ff.

The Sayings are as follows :—

I had the fear of God as the guide of my journey
through Gaul and Italy and, moreover, in the islands which
are in the Tyrrhene Sea.

Ye departed from the world to Paradise. Thanks be to
God.

Church of the Scots! nay, of the Romans! In order
that ye be Christians as well as Romans ye must chant in
your churches at every hour of prayer that glorious word,
Kyrie eleison, Christe eleison. Let every church that follows
me chant *Kyrie eleison, Christe eleison.*

Thanks be to God.

INTRODUCTION TO MUIRCHU'S LIFE OF ST. PATRICK

THE Life of St. Patrick, a translation of which is here printed, is the most ancient Life of the Saint now extant. The first book, at least, must have been published before A.D. 699; for Bishop Ædh, to whom it is dedicated, died in that year. There is, however, another document dealing with St. Patrick's life, which is probably earlier, viz. The Memoranda of Bishop Tirechán, dated by Prof. Bury between A.D. 664 and 668 (*St. Patrick*, p. 248). This work, although of considerable interest and historical value, is not a *Life* in the strict sense. See Introduction, p. 24.

Muirchu's work has come down to us in two MSS., neither of which is perfect; but, as one possesses what the other lacks, the whole *Life* is accessible to the modern reader.

1. The Book of Armagh, folios 2-8, 20. The date of this MS. is between A D. 807 and A.D. 846; it is cited here as A.

2 MS. No. 64 in the Royal Library of Brussels, which was published in 1882 by the Rev. E. Hogan, S.J., in *Analecta Bollandiana*, i, p. 531. Father Hogan dates this MS. not earlier than the eleventh century. It is cited here as B.

The scribe of A used two exemplars, from one of which (A2) he copied chapters 1-26 of Book i. (Book i in A2 contained apparently no more than twenty-six chapters), and the whole of Book ii. Folio 1 of A, however, has been lost, and the first extant leaf begins early in chapter 7. From the other exemplar (A1) he copied, on folio 20 of his MS., the Preface and Table of Contents of Book i.

In this translation the twenty-nine chapters into which Book i. is divided are given in the order presented in that

Table; and the titles, as given in the Table, are prefixed to the several chapters. This order is that in which, most probably, the chapters stood in the copy of the *Life* presented by Muirchu to Bishop Ædh. The note placed here at the close of Book i. follows the Table in A (fol. 20, v° *a*). This note strongly suggests that Book i. embodies the whole of the tradition that came to Muirchu through Bishop Ædh.

But when the content of Book ii. is added to that of Book i., a rearrangement of the whole material seems to become desirable; and in fact such a rearrangement is presented in B.

Chapters 1–22 of Book i. form a connected story—the beginning of Patrick's missionary work in Ireland. But chapters 23–29 have no connexion with what precedes them or with each other; they might without inconvenience be put in any order, as so many examples of the "signs following" referred to at the close of chapter 22.

Consequently, the editor of the exemplar copied in B made Book i. end with chapter 22; but he assigned 23 chapters to Book i., by inserting the last chapter of Book ii. (chapter 15) between chapters 12 and 13 of Book i. He omitted chapter 26 of Book i. ("Of the fruitful land turned into a salt marsh"), probably thinking it superfluous, inasmuch as a similar miracle is related in chapter 25.

The following Table exhibits the difference in order between A1 and B, as far as B is extant :—

A1		B
i. 23	=	ii. 4
24		6
25		5
26		om.
27		1
28		3
29		2

Unfortunately, B breaks off in the middle of chapter 24 (A), so that we cannot be sure as to his disposition of the rest of the material, viz. Book ii. chapters 1–14 (A2). His insertion of chapter 15 into Book i. has been noticed above.

The Book of Armagh never contained the text of chapters 27, 28, 29 of Book i., although the titles are preserved in the Table on fol. 20. For these chapters, as well as for chapters 1–6, B is our sole authority. The introductory clause in chapter 27 is certainly an interpolation by the editor of the exemplar copied in B. It is to be noted that Probus, the author of the *Vita Quinta*, who wrote "not much earlier than the middle of the tenth century" (Bury, *op. cit.* p. 274), agrees with B in its division of the books.

The translation here given is based, as far as possible, on the text of A, but occasionally the readings of B and of *Vitæ* ii. iv. and v., which are partly based on Muirchu, have been silently adopted. One or two recent emendations of the text are indicated in the notes.

The full name of the author of this Life, as given in the note appended to the Table of Contents of Book i. (printed here at the end of that book) was Muirchu-maccu-Machtheni, *i. e.* Muirchu son of Machthene. In the Preface he gives his father's name as Cogitosus. Bishop Graves' emendation, *Coguitosi* for *cognito si*, is now generally accepted. The spelling *ui* for *i* has many analogies in the Book of Armagh. The name itself, *Cogitosus*, is supposed to be a Latinization of *Machthene*, as though the latter were derived from the Irish *machtaigim*, "I consider with wonder" (see Gwynn, *op. cit.* p. xix.; Bury, *St. Patrick*, p. 255). Cogitosus is known as the author of a Life of St. Brigid of Kildare; and Muirchu claims that in his attempt to write the Life of a great saint, he is following in his father's footsteps.

Muirchu was a Leinster man. This is strongly suggested

by his father's association with Kildare, and his own intimate connexion with Ædh, bishop of Sleibte (Sletty), on the borders of Co. Carlow. Both Ædh and Muirchu subscribed the Acts of the Synod held at Birr, by Adamnan, A.D. 695–697.

There is evidence that Ædh visited Armagh, and made a formal submission to the primatial claims of its bishop; and it is probable that Muirchu's Life, which deals almost exclusively with St. Patrick's work in the north of Ireland, was inspired by a desire to offer a literary tribute from Leinster to Armagh.

It is to be noted that Muirchu exhibits familiarity with the Hymn of St. Sechnall in Book i. 7, 11, Book ii. 1.

PREFACE

FORASMUCH as many, my Lord Ædh, have taken in hand
to set forth in order a declaration according to that which
their fathers and those who from the beginning were
ministers of the word delivered unto them—— But these
writers never attained to one sure track of history, on
account of the extreme difficulty of the task of story-telling,
and because of conflicting opinions, and the very many
surmises of very many persons. Therefore, if I mistake
not, as our popular proverb has it, " Like bringing boys
into a council meeting," I have brought the infantile row-
boat of my feeble brain into this most dangerous and deep
ocean of sacred story, where mountainous seas rage and
swell, amidst sharpest rocks lying in unknown seas, an ocean
on which no boat has as yet ventured, save only that of my
father Cogitosus.   However, that I seem not to make a great
thing out of what is small, I shall assay, in obedience to the
command of thy holiness and authority, to unfold, piece-
meal and with difficulty, these few out of the many actions
of St. Patrick. My skill is small; my authorities are
uncertain [*or*, anonymous]; my memory is treacherous;
my intelligence is worn out; my style is poor; yet the
feeling of my love is most pious.

BOOK I

CHAPTER I

OF THE BIRTH OF PATRICK AND OF HIS FIRST CAPTIVITY

PATRICK, who was also called Sochet, was of the British race and born in Britain. He was the son of Cualfarnus a deacon, who, as he tells us himself, was the son of Potitus a presbyter, who belonged to the town of Bannavem Thaburinde, not far distant from our sea. We have ascertained repeatedly that this town is unquestionably Ventre. Moreover his mother's name was Concessa.

When a lad sixteen years old, he was with others carried captive into this island of barbarians, and was kept in slavery in the house of a certain chieftain, a heathen man and a harsh. [He spent] six years [in that captivity], as was the custom of the Hebrews; [he lived] in the fear and dread of God, according to the maxim of the Psalmist, in many watchings and prayers. He used to pray a hundred times in the day-time, and a hundred times during the night, gladly rendering [to God the things that are God's], and beginning to fear God and to love the Almighty Lord; for up to that time he had been ignorant of the true God; but then the spirit was fervent within him. [Finally], after many tribulations there [endured], after suffering hunger and thirst, cold and nakedness, after the work of tending cattle, after visits from the angel Victoricus who was sent to him from God, after great miracles which are known to nearly everybody, after answers from God (of which I shall cite only the one or two following, as examples : " Thou fastest to good purpose, thou who art soon to go to thy native land," and, " Lo, thy ship is ready." The ship, however, was not near at hand, but was distant about two hundred miles, in a place to which he had never fared) ; after all these things, as we have said, things which it is scarcely possible for any one to reckon up, he forsook the cruel heathen man and his works, and sailed to Britain in the twenty-third year of his age in the ship made ready for him, with strange, barbarous and heathen men who worshipped many false gods ; yet taking into holy companionship the heavenly and everlasting God.

CHAPTER II

OF HIS VOYAGE WITH THE HEATHEN, AND HIS SUFFERINGS IN THE DESERT. OF THE FOOD PROVIDENTIALLY BROUGHT TO HIM AND TO THE HEATHEN

AND so for three days and as many nights, like Jonah, he was storm-tossed with the ungodly; and after that, for twenty-eight days he had a weary journey through the desert—like Moses, and yet unlike him—the heathens, who were well nigh perishing from hunger and thirst, murmuring as did the Jews. He was urged and tempted by the shipmaster, and he was requested that he should pray to his God for them, lest they should perish ; he was prevailed on by mortals; he had compassion on the multitude ; he was troubled in spirit, crowned for his worthiness, magnified by God ; he supplied to them abundance of food from the herd of swine sent to him by God, as [the Israelites of old were supplied] from the flock of quails, by the help of God.

There was wild honey, too, such as once supplied the needs of John. But while John used locusts, swine's flesh was substituted, in accordance with their deserts, for these vile heathen. But the holy Patrick tasted nought of this food, for it had been offered in sacrifice to idols; yet he remained unharmed, neither hungry nor thirsty. But while he was asleep the same night, Satan assailed him sorely, fashioning huge rocks, and [with them] crushing his limbs; but he called twice upon Helias; and the sun rose upon him, and with its beams drove away all the mists of darkness, and his strength came back to him.

CHAPTER III

OF THE SECOND CAPTIVITY WHICH HE ENDURED FOR SIXTY DAYS AT THE HANDS OF HIS ENEMIES

AND again, after many years, he suffered captivity at the hands of foreigners. This time, on the first night, it was vouchsafed to him to hear an answer from God: "For two months thou shalt be with them, that is, with thine enemies." And so it came to pass; for on the sixtieth day the Lord delivered him out of their hands, and provided for him and his companions, food and fire and shelter, until on the tenth day they reached human habitations.

CHAPTER IV

OF HIS RECEPTION BY HIS RELATIVES, WHEN THEY RECOGNIZED HIM

AND again, after a few years, he found rest as beforetime in his own native land with his relatives, who received him as a son; and they entreated him, that after such tribulations and trials, he should never leave them for the rest of his life. But he consented not. And there many visions were shewn to him.

F

CHAPTER V

OF HIS AGE WHEN, GOING TO VISIT THE APOSTOLIC SEE, HE DESIRED TO LEARN WISDOM

AND he was thirty years of age, [having grown], as the Apostle says, "into a perfect man, into the measure of the age of the fulness of Christ." He set forth then to visit and pay his respects to the Apostolic See, the head of all the churches of the whole world, as one that was already wise in sacred mysteries to which God had called him, to learn and understand and fulfil them ; and that he should preach and impart the grace of God to foreign nations, converting them to the faith of Christ.

CHAPTER VI

OF HOW HE FOUND ST. GERMANUS IN GAUL, AND THEREFORE WENT NO FURTHER

AND so he crossed the southern British sea, and began his journey, intending to cross by the Gallic Alps to the furthest point, as he had purposed in his heart; when he found—the choicest gift [of God]—a certain very holy bishop, Germanus, ruling in his city of Alsiodorum.

With him he stayed no little time, just as Paul sat at the feet of Gamaliel ; and in all submissiveness, patience and obedience, he learnt, loved and kept, with all the desire of his mind, knowledge, wisdom, chastity and everything that is profitable to the spirit and the soul, with great fear and love of God, in goodness and singleness of heart, a virgin in body and mind alike.

CHAPTER VII

OF HIS AGE WHEN THE ANGEL VISITED HIM, TO THE END THAT HE MIGHT COME HITHER

WHEN he had spent there a long time, which some reckon as forty years, some as thirty, that ancient and very trusty one, named Victoricus, who,[1] when he was in slavery in Ireland, had told him all things before they came to pass, visited him in frequent visions, saying that the time had arrived for him to go, and with the Gospel net fish for the wild and savage tribes to whom God had sent him to teach them. And there it was said to him in a vision, "The boys and girls of the Wood of Fochlath are calling thee," and so forth.

CHAPTER VIII

OF HIS RETURN FROM GAUL, AND OF THE CONSECRATION OF PALLADIUS AND HIS DEATH SOON AFTERWARDS

AT the bidding therefore of a fitting occasion, and accompanied by his divine helper, he sets forth on the journey which he had begun to the work for which he had long since been prepared, the work, to wit, of the Gospel. And Germanus sent an elder with him, that is, Segitius a presbyter, that he might have a witness and a companion, because he had not yet been ordained to pontifical rank by the holy lord Germanus. For they knew that Palladius, the archdeacon of Pope Celestinus, bishop of the city of Rome, who then held the Apostolic See, the forty-fifth from Saint Peter the Apostle, [they knew, I say, that] Palladius had been consecrated and sent to convert this island lying under the rigour of winter.

But God prohibited him; because no one can receive anything from earth unless it were given to him from heaven. For neither did those wild and rough people readily receive his teaching, nor did he himself desire to spend a long time in a land not his own; but he returned to him that sent him. Returning then hence, he crossed the first sea; and, continuing his journey by land, he died n the country of the Britons.

[1] A begins.

CHAPTER IX

OF HIS CONSECRATION BY BISHOP AMATHOREX AFTER PALLADIUS WAS DEAD

WHEN tidings came of the death of St. Palladius in Britain (because the disciples of Palladius, viz. Augustinus and Benedictus and the rest, returned and told in Ebmoria of his death), Patrick and they who were with him turned aside to a certain famous man, a chief bishop, Amathorex by name, who dwelt in the neighbourhood. And there St. Patrick, knowing the things that were to happen to him, received the episcopal rank from Amathorex, the holy bishop. Moreover, Auxilius and Iserninus and others received lower degrees of the ministry on the same day that Patrick was consecrated.

Then, having received the benedictions, and all things having been accomplished according to custom (moreover with a special appropriateness to Patrick, this verse of the Psalmist was sung, "Thou art a priest for ever, after the order of Melchizedek"), the venerable traveller got on board, in the name of the Blessed Trinity, a ship prepared for him, and arrived in Britain ; and dispensing with everything that could delay his journey [on foot], except what the requirements of ordinary life demand (for no one seeks the Lord by sloth), with all speed and with a favouring wind, he crossed our sea.

CHAPTER X

OF THE HEATHEN KING WHO DWELT IN TEMORIA, WHEN ST. PATRICK CAME BRINGING BAPTISM

Now in the days in which these things happened, there was in the aforesaid country a certain great king, a fierce and heathen High-King of barbarians, reigning in Temoria, which was the capital of the kingdom of the Irish, Loiguire by name, the son of Neill, who is the ancestor of the royal stock of almost the whole of this island.

Now he had about him wise men and magicians and augurs and enchanters and inventors of every evil art, who through their heathenish and idolatrous religion had skill to know and foresee all things before they came to pass. And of these there were two who were preferred beyond the others, whose names were, Lothroch, otherwise Lochru, and Lucetmael, otherwise Ronal. And these two by their magical arts frequently foretold the coming of a certain foreign religion, in the manner of a kingdom, with a certain strange and harmful doctrine, brought from a long distance across the seas, proclaimed by a few, accepted by the many, and honoured by all; one that would overturn kingdoms, slay kings that resist it, lead away multitudes, destroy all their gods, and, having cast down all the resources of their art, reign for ever and ever.

Moreover they indicated him who should bear and advocate this religion. And they prophesied in the following words cast into poetical form, words frequently uttered by them, more especially in the two or three years which preceded the coming of Patrick. Now these are the words of the poem, which are somewhat obscure, on account of the idiom of the language.

> "Adze-head will come
> With his crook-headed staff,
> And his house [chasuble] holed for his head
> He will chant impiety from his table in the east of his house.
> His whole household will respond to him. So be it, So be it."

Which can be more plainly expressed in our language [1] When therefore all these things come to pass, our kingdom, which is a heathen one, will not stand.

And so it afterwards came to pass. For the worship of idols having been overturned on the coming of Patrick, the faith of Christ—our Catholic faith—filled the whole land. But let this suffice on this matter. Let us return to our subject.

[1] Here probably the Irish form of the prophecy originally stood.

CHAPTER XI

OF HIS FIRST JOURNEY IN THIS ISLAND, TO THE END THAT
HE MIGHT RANSOM HIMSELF FROM MILIUCC BEFORE HE
RESCUED OTHERS FROM THE DEVIL

So, the holy voyage having been finished and completed,
the ship of the Saint, laded with wonderful and spiritual
treasures from beyond the seas, was borne, as to a convenient harbour, to the country of the Coolenni, to a
harbour famous in our country, which is called the Mouth
of the Dee.

And when here, it seemed to him that there was nothing
better for him to do than to ransom himself in the first
instance. So he sought thence the north country, carrying
a twofold ransom from slavery—to wit, an earthly and a
heavenly—to that heathen man Miliucc, in whose house
he had once lived in captivity, that he might deliver from
captivity him whom he had formerly served as a captive.

So he turned the prow of his ship to the most easterly
island which to this day is called by his name. Proceeding thence he left Breg and the Conaille country,
and also the Ulaid country on the left, and he entered the
furthest point of a lough which is Brene. And he and
they that were with him in the ship landed at the mouth of
the Slain And they hid their skiff, and went a very short
distance into the country to rest there. And a swineherd
discovered them; he belonged to a certain man named
Dichu, who, although a heathen, was of a good natural
disposition. He lived in a place which is now known by
the name of Patrick's Barn. Now the swineherd, supposing
that they were thieves and robbers, went and told his
master Dichu, and brought him upon them without their
being aware of it. Now he had purposed in his heart to
slay them; but when he beheld the countenance of St.
Patrick, the Lord turned his thoughts to good. And

Patrick preached the faith to him ; and there he believed in Patrick before any one else did ; and there the Saint rested with him not many days.

But wishing to go with all speed to visit the aforesaid Miliucc, and bring him his ransom, and thus convert him to the faith of Christ, he left his ship in charge of Dichu, and began a land journey into the country of the Cruidneni, until he reached Mount Mis. Now, long before, in the time when he was a captive slave, he saw the angel Victoricus ascend from this mountain into heaven in his sight, with hurried step, leaving the print of his foot on the rock of a second mountain.

CHAPTER XII

ON THE DEATH OF MILIUCC, AND PATRICK'S WORDS CONCERNING HIS POSTERITY

Now when Miliucc heard that his slave was coming to see him, to the end that he should, at the close of his life, adopt, as it were by force, a religion which he disliked, [fearing] lest he should be in subjection to a slave, and that he [the slave] should lord it over him, he committed himself to the flames, at the instigation of the devil and of his own accord. Having collected around him every article of his property, he was burnt up in the house in which he had lived as king.

Now St. Patrick was standing in the aforesaid place on the southern side of Mount Mis, where, coming with such gracious purpose, he first caught sight of the country where he had been a slave, a spot which is now marked by a cross ; and at the first view of that country, there, under his eyes, he beheld the burning pyre of the king.

And so, stupefied at this deed, he spake not a word for two or three hours. And then with sighs and tears and groans he uttered these words, and said, I know not ; God knoweth. As for this king man who hath committed himself to the flames, lest he should become a believer at the close of his life, and serve the everlasting God—I know not ; God knoweth ;—none of his sons shall sit as king upon the throne of his kingdom from generation to generation ; moreover his seed shall be in servitude for evermore.

Having said this, he prayed and armed himself with the sign of the cross ; and quickly bent his steps to the country of the Ulaid, by the same way that he had come, and arrived again at the Plain of Inis, to Dichu ; and there he stayed many days ; and he went round the whole country-side, and chose [clergymen], and did deeds of love ; and there the faith began to grow.

CHAPTER XIII

OF THE ADVICE OF ST. PATRICK WHEN DELIBERATING ABOUT THE CELEBRATION OF THE FIRST PASSOVER

Now in those days the Passover drew near, which was the first Passover celebrated to God in the Egypt of this island, as once it was [celebrated] in Goshen.

And they took counsel as to where they should celebrate the first Passover amongst the nations to whom God had sent them. And when many suggestions had been thrown out on this subject, at last it seemed good to Saint Patrick, inspired by God as he was, that this great feast of the Lord, which is the chief of all feasts, should be celebrated in the great plain where was the chiefest kingdom of those tribes, which was the head of all heathenism and idolatry ; that this unconquered wedge should be driven at the outset into the head of all idolatry, by the mallet of a mighty work joined with faith, [wielded] by the spiritual hands of St. Patrick and his companions, so that it should never more be able to rise against the faith of Christ. And so it came to pass.

CHAPTER XIV

OF THE FIRST PASCHAL SACRIFICE THAT WAS MADE IN THIS ISLAND

So they carried down their boat to the sea, and left the good man Dichu in full faith and peace. They departed from the Plain of Inis; and leaving on the right hand everything which had before been, naturally, on the left, [and leaving the spiritual care of them] to the [future] fulfilment of their ministry, they were borne well and prosperously to the harbour of the Mouth of the Colpdi. And leaving the ship there, they proceeded on foot to the aforesaid great plain, until at last at evening, they reached The Graves of the Men of Fecc [Fiacc], which, as the story goes, was dug by the men, that is the slaves, of Feccol Ferchertni, who was one of the nine great prophets of Breg. And having pitched his tent there, St. Patrick with his companions paid to the most high God the due vows of the Paschal feast and the sacrifice of praise with all devotion, according to the words of the prophet.

CHAPTER XV

OF THE HEATHEN FEAST AT TEMORIA THE SAME NIGHT ON WHICH ST. PATRICK WAS ENGAGED IN HIS PASCHAL WORSHIP

Now it happened that in that year the heathen were wont to celebrate an idolatrous feast with many incantations and magical devices, and other superstitions of idolatry. And there were also gathered together kings, satraps, leaders, princes and chief men of the people; and, moreover, magicians and enchanters and augurs and those who sought out and taught every art and every wile were called to

Loiguire, as once upon a time to King Nebuchadrezzar, to Temoria, their Babylon.

And it was on the same night that St. Patrick was observing the Paschal feast that they were celebrating their heathen festival. Moreover there was a custom amongst them, made know to all by an edict, that whoever in the whole district, whether far off or near, should in that night kindle a fire before one should have been lighted in the royal house, that is, in the palace of Temoria, his soul should be cut off from among his people.

Accordingly Saint Patrick, in his celebration of the holy Paschal feast, kindled a divine fire, very bright and blessed, which as it shone forth at night, was seen by almost all the dwellers in the plain.

Accordingly it happened that it was seen from Temoria; and when it was seen, all beheld it and were amazed. And when all the nobles and elders and magicians had been gathered together, the king said to them, What is this? Who is it that has dared to do this impiety in my kingdom? Let him die the death! And all the nobles and elders made answer, We know not who has done this thing. Then the magicians answered and said, O king, live for ever. As for this fire which we behold, and which has been lighted up this night before one was lighted in thy house, that is, in the palace of Temoria, unless it be put out on this night on which it has been lighted up, it will not be put out for ever. Moreover it will overcome all the fires of our religion. And he who kindled it, and the kingdom that will follow, from which it is kindled this night, will overcome both all of us and thee too, and it will draw away all the men of thy kingdom, and all kingdoms will yield to it, and he will fill all things, and will reign for ever and ever.

CHAPTER XVI

OF KING LOIGUIRE'S MARCH FROM TEMORIA TO PATRICK
ON THE PASCHAL NIGHT

WHEN king Loiguire had heard these things, he was, like, Herod of old, sore troubled, and all the city of Temoria with him. And he answered and said, It shall not be so ; but now we will go that we may see the issue of the matter , and we shall take and slay those who do such an impiety against our kingdom.

And so, having yoked nine chariots, in accordance with the tradition of the gods, and taking with him for the conflict those two magicians who excelled all others, that is to say, Lucetmael and Lochru, Loiguire proceeded at the close of that night from Temoria to The Graves of the Men of Fecc, turning the faces of the men and of the horses to the left, in accordance with their notion of what is fitting [in such a case.]

And as they went on their way, the magicians said to the king, O king, thou must not go into the place in which the fire is, lest afterwards perchance thou worship him who kindled it ; but thou must be outside it, near at hand ; and he will be summoned to thee, that he may worship thee and thou have dominion over him [or be owned as lord]. And we and he shall parley with one another in thy presence, O king ; and in this way thou wilt test us. And the king answered and said, Ye have advised well ; I will do as ye have said. And when they arrived at the appointed place, they alighted from their chariots and horses ; and they entered not into the enclosure of the place where the fire had been kindled ; but took their seats close by.

CHAPTER XVII

HOW PATRICK WAS CALLED TO THE KING; OF THE FAITH OF ERCC SON OF DAIG; OF THE DEATH OF THE MAGICIAN THAT NIGHT

AND St. Patrick was called to the king outside the place where the fire had been kindled. And the magicians said to their people, Let us not rise up at the approach of this fellow; for whosoever rises up at the approach of this fellow will afterwards believe in him and worship him.

At last St. Patrick rose, and when he saw their many chariots and horses, he came to them, singing with voice and heart, very appropriately, the following verse of the Psalmist. "Some put their trust in chariots and some in horses; but we will walk in the name of the Lord our God." They, however, did not rise at his approach. But only one, helped by the Lord, who willed not to obey the words of the magicians, rose up. This was Ercc the son of Daig, whose relics are now venerated in the city called Slane. And Patrick blessed him; and he believed in the everlasting God.

And when they began to parley with one another, the second magician, named Lochru, was insolent in the Saint's presence, and had the audacity with swelling words to disparage the Catholic faith. As he uttered such things, Saint Patrick regarded him with a stern glance, as Peter once looked on Simon; and powerfully, with a loud voice, he confidently addressed the Lord and said, O Lord, who canst do all things, and in whose power all things hold together, and who hast sent me hither—as for this impious man who blasphemes Thy name, let him now be taken up out of this and die speedily. And when he had thus spoken, the magician was caught up into the air, and then let fall from above, and, his skull striking on a rock, he was dashed to pieces and killed before their faces; and the heathen folk were dismayed.

CHAPTER XVIII

OF THE WRATH OF THE KING AND HIS PEOPLE AGAINST PATRICK, AND OF THE STROKE OF GOD UPON THEM, AND OF THE TRANSFORMATION OF PATRICK IN THE PRESENCE OF THE HEATHEN

Now the king with his people, enraged with Patrick on account of this thing, was minded to slay him, and said, Lay hands on this fellow who is destroying us. Then St. Patrick, seeing that the ungodly heathen folk were about to rush upon him, rose up, and with a clear voice said, "Let God arise, and let his enemies be scattered; let them also that hate him flee before him." And straightway darkness came down, and a certain horrible commotion arose, and the ungodly men fought amongst themselves, one rising up against another, and there was a great earthquake, "and He bound the axles of their chariots, and drove them with violence," and they rushed in headlong flight —both chariots and horses—over the level ground of the great plain, till at last only a few of them escaped half alive to the mountain of Monduirn; and, at the curse of Patrick, seven times seven men were laid low by this stroke in the presence of the king and his elders, until there remained only himself and his wife and two others of his companions; and they were sore afraid. So the queen approached Patrick and said to him, O man, righteous and mighty, do not destroy the king; for the king will come and kneel and worship thy Lord. And the king, compelled by fear, came and knelt before the Saint, and feigned to worship Him whom he did not wish to worship.

And when they had parted from one another, the king went a little way, and called St. Patrick with feigned words, minding to slay him by some means. But St. Patrick, knowing the thoughts of the villainous king, blessed his companions (eight men and a lad) in the name of Jesus Christ, and came to the king. The king counted them as they came; and straightway they were nowhere to be seen, taken away from the king's sight; but the heathen folk saw nought but eight stags and a fawn going as it were to the wilderness. And king Loiguire, with the few that had escaped, returned at dawn to Temoria sad, cowed and humiliated.

CHAPTER XIX

HOW PATRICK CAME TO TEMORIA ON EASTER DAY, AND OF THE FAITH OF DUBTHACH-MACCU-LUGIR

Now on the next day, that is, the day of the Paschal feast, the kings and princes and magicians of all Ireland were sitting at meat in Loiguire's house, for it was the chiefest of their festivals. And as they were eating and drinking wine in the palace of Temoria, and some were talking and others thinking of the things which had come to pass, St. Patrick came, with five men only—the doors being shut, like as we read about Christ—to contend for the holy faith, and preach the word of God in Temoria before all the tribes of the Irish people there gathered together.

When therefore he entered the banqueting hall of Temoria, no one of them all rose up at his approach save one only, and that was Dubthach-maccu-Lugir, an excellent poet, with whom there was staying at that time a certain young poet named Fiacc, who afterwards became a famous bishop, and whose relics are now venerated at Sleibti.

This Dubthach, as I have said, alone of the heathen folk, rose up in honour of St. Patrick; and the Saint blessed him, and he was the first to believe in God that day; and it was counted unto him for righteousness.

So when Patrick appeared, he was invited by the heathen to partake of food, that they might prove him in respect of things that should come to pass. He, however, knowing the things that should come to pass, did not refuse to eat.

CHAPTER XX

OF THE CONTEST OF PATRICK WITH THE MAGICIAN ON THAT DAY, AND OF HIS WONDERFUL MIRACLES

Now while all were feasting, the magician Lucetmael, who had taken part in the contest at night, was eager, even that day when his comrade was dead, to contend with St. Patrick. And, to make a beginning of the matter, he put, while the others were looking, somewhat from his own vessel into Patrick's cup, to try what he would do. St. Patrick, perceiving the kind of trial intended, blessed his cup in the sight of all; and, lo, the liquor was turned into ice. And when he had turned the vessel upside down, that drop only fell out which the magician had put into it. And he blessed his cup again, and the liquor was restored to its own nature; and all marvelled.

And after [the trial of] the cup, the magician said, Let us work miracles on this great plain. And Patrick answered and said, What miracles? And the magician said, Let us bring snow upon the earth. Then said Patrick, I do not wish to bring things that are contrary to the will of God. And the magician said, I shall bring it in the sight of all. Then he began his magical incantations, and brought down snow over the whole plain to the depth of a man's waist; and all saw it and marvelled. And St. Patrick said, Lo, we see this thing; now take it away. And he said, I cannot take it away till this time to-morrow. And the Saint said, Thou art able to do evil, but not good; I am not of that sort. Then he blessed the whole plain round about; and the snow vanished quicker than a word could be uttered, without any rain or cloud or wind. And the multitude shouted aloud, and marvelled greatly.

And a little after this, the magician invoked his demons, and brought upon the earth a very thick darkness, as a miracle; and all murmured at it. And the Saint said, Drive away the darkness. But he could not in this case either. St. Patrick however prayed and uttered a blessing, and suddenly the darkness was driven away, and the sun shone forth. And all shouted aloud and gave thanks.

Now when all these things had been done by the magician and Patrick, in the sight of the king, the king said to them, Throw your books into water; and we shall worship him whose books come out unharmed. Patrick replied, I will do it. But the magician said, I do not wish to enter into a trial by water with this fellow; for water is his God. He had evidently heard of baptism by water given by Patrick. And the king answered and said, Throw them into fire. And Patrick said, I am ready. But the magician, being unwilling, said, This man worships as his God water and fire turn about every alternate year. And the Saint said, That is not so, but thou thyself shalt go, and one of my lads shall go with thee, into a house separated and shut up; and my garment shall be around thee, and thy garment around me, and thus shall ye together be set on fire; and ye shall be judged in the sight of the Most High.

And this suggestion was adopted; and a house was built for them, whereof one half was built of green wood and the other half of dry. And the magician was put into the part of the house made of green wood; and one of Saint Patrick's lads, named Benineus, was put with a magician's robe into the part that was made of dry wood. The house was then shut up from the outside, and set on fire before the whole multitude. And it came to pass in that hour, that as Patrick prayed, the flame of the fire burnt up the magician with the half of the house that was made of green wood, the cloak of Saint Patrick only remaining whole, inasmuch as the fire did not touch it. Benineus, on the other hand, was fortunate with the half of the house that was made of dry wood; for, as it is told about The Three Children, the fire did not touch him at all; nor was he alarmed, nor did it do him any harm; only the cloak of the magician which was around him was, by the will of God, burnt up.

And the king was greatly enraged against Patrick, because of the death of his magician, and he almost rushed upon him, minding to slay him; but God hindered him. For at the prayer of Patrick and at his cry, the wrath of God fell upon the ungodly people, and many of them perished. And St. Patrick said to the king, Unless thou believest now, thou shalt die speedily, because the wrath of God will fall upon thy head. And the king feared exceedingly, "and his heart was moved," and his whole city with him.

CHAPTER XXI

OF THE CONVERSION OF KING LOIGUIRE, AND OF THE WORDS OF PATRICK CONCERNING HIS KINGDOM AFTER HIM

AND so when the elders and all his senate were gathered together, King Loiguire said to them, It is better for me to believe than to die. And after taking counsel, he believed on that day, by the advice of his friends, and turned to the everlasting Lord God of Israel; and there many others believed as well. And St. Patrick said to the king, Because thou didst withstand my teaching, and wast a stumbling-block to me, although the days of thy reign shall be prolonged, nevertheless none of thy seed shall be king for ever.

CHAPTER XXII

OF THE TEACHING, AND BAPTISM AND MIRACLES OF ST. PATRICK, AFTER THE EXAMPLE OF CHRIST

Now St. Patrick, according to the command of the Lord Jesus, to "go and teach all nations, baptizing them in the

G

name of the Father and of the Son and of the Holy
Ghost," set out from Temoria and preached, "the Lord
working with him, and confirming the word with signs
following."

CHAPTER XXIII

OF MACCUIL AND HIS CONVERSION AT THE WORD
PREACHED BY PATRICK

IN Patrick's time there lived in the country of the Ulaid
folk a certain man named Maccuil-maccu-Greccæ; and this
man was such a very ungodly, savage tyrant, that he was
called Cyclops. He was depraved in his thoughts, violent
in his words, malicious in his deeds, bitter in spirit,
wrathful in disposition, villainous in body, cruel in mind,
heathenish in life, monstrous in conscience, inclining to
such a depth of ungodliness, that one day [he acted as
follows].

There is a mountainous place, rugged and steep, in
Druimm-maccu-Echaid, where he daily practised his tyranny,
taking the vilest signs of cruelty, and slaying in cruel fashion
strangers that passed by.

Now, one day, when he was sitting at this place, he saw
St. Patrick radiating with the clear light of faith, and
resplendent with a certain wonderful diadem of heavenly
glory; he saw him, I say, walking, with unshaken confidence
of doctrine, on a road agreeable thereto. And he thought
to slay him, and said to his followers, Lo, here comes that
deceiver and perverter of mankind, whose wont it is to do
juggling tricks, that he may deceive and beguile many.
Let us now go and test him, and we shall know if that God
of whom he makes boast has any power.

And so they tested the holy man in the following way .—

They placed one of their own number, who was in good health, in their midst covered with a blanket, feigning to be sick unto death, that they might test the Saint by a trick of this kind; calling the holy man a deceiver, his miracles jugglery, and his prayers charms and incantations.

When St. Patrick with his disciples came up, the heathen folk said to him, Lo, one of us is now sick; come then, and chant over him some of the spells of thy religion, if perchance he may be healed. St. Patrick, however, knowing all their deceits and tricks, said boldly and fearlessly, It is no wonder he is sick. And when his companions uncovered the face of the man who was feigning sickness, they perceived that he was already dead. And they, confounded and wondering at such a miracle, said one to another with groans, Truly this is a man of God; we have done ill in testing him.

But St. Patrick, turning to Maccuil, said, Wherefore didst thou wish to test me? That cruel tyrant answered and said, I am sorry for having done this; and I shall do whatsoever thou biddest me; and I hand myself over now into the power of thy most high God whom thou preachest. And the Saint said, Believe then in my God, the Lord Jesus, and confess thy sins and be baptized in the name of the Father and of the Son and of the Holy Ghost. And he was converted in that hour, and believed in the everlasting God.

Moreover he was baptized. And Maccuil proceeded to say, I confess to thee, my holy lord Patrick, that I purposed to slay thee; give sentence therefore what punishment is due for a crime so great and of such a nature. And Patrick said, I cannot judge; but God will judge. Nevertheless, do thou now go forth unarmed to the sea, and depart quickly from this Irish land, taking nothing with thee of thy property save a cheap and small garment to cover thy body. Eat and drink nothing of the produce of this island;

bear a mark of thy sin on thy head; and after thou hast reached the sea, lock thy feet together with an iron fetter, and throw the key of it into the sea. Place thyself in a boat made of a single hide, without either rudder or oars, and be ready to go whithersoever the wind and the waves may lead thee; and whatsoever land Divine Providence may bear thee to, dwell in it, and there practise obedience to the commandments of God. And Maccuil said, I shall do as thou hast said. But what shall we do about the dead man? And Patrick said, He will live and rise again without pain. So Patrick raised him up in that same hour, and he lived again in good health.

And Maccuil departed thence as quickly as possible to the sea that is south of the Plain of Inis, possessing the unshaken confidence of faith. And he locked himself together on the shore, and threw the key into the sea, as he had been instructed; and he put to sea in a little boat; and the north wind blew on him, and bore him southwards, and cast him on an island named Evonia. And there he found two men, very famous, resplendent in faith and learning, who were the first to teach the word of God and baptism in Evonia And the inhabitants of that island were, through their teaching, converted to the Catholic faith. Their names are Conindri and Rumili.

Now they, when they beheld a man dressed in only one garment, were amazed, and had pity on him, and drew him out of the sea, and received him with joy. He then, in a country allotted to him by God, where he found spiritual fathers, practised both his body and soul in their rule; and passed the whole time of his life with those two holy bishops, until he was made their successor in the episcopate. This is Maccuil, Bishop of Man and prelate of Arddæ Huimnonn.

CHAPTER XXIV

OF THE STORY OF DAIRE, AND OF THE HORSE, AND OF THE PRESENTATION OF ARDD-MACHÆ TO PATRICK

THERE was in the country of Airthir a certain rich and honourable man named Daire. To him Patrick made request that he would grant him some place for the exercise of religion. And the rich man said to the Saint, What place dost thou desire? I desire, said the Saint, that thou grant me that high ground which is called The Ridge of the Willow; and I shall build there a place. But he was unwilling to give the Saint that high ground, but he gave him another place on lower ground, where is now The Graves [or The Church] of the Relics, near Ardd-Machæ; and there St. Patrick dwelt with his people.

Now some time after, there came a groom of Daire's, leading his admirable horse, to graze on the grass land of the Christians. And Patrick was offended at the horse trespassing in this way on his ground; and he said, Daire has done a foolish thing in sending brute beasts to disturb the little holy place which he gave to God. But the groom was "like a deaf man and heard not, and as one that is dumb who doth not open his mouth;" he said nothing, but went away, leaving the horse there for the night. But on the next day, when the groom came in the morning to see his horse, he found it dead already. So he went back home in grief, and said to his lord, See, that Christian has killed thy horse; he was annoyed at the disturbance of his place. And Daire said, Let him be slain too; go ye now and kill him.

And as they were going forth, a death stroke, quicker than a word, fell on Daire. And his wife said, This death stroke is on account of the Christian. Let some one go quickly, and let his good offices [or, blessing] be brought to us, and thou wilt be cured; and let those who went forth to kill him be forbidden to do so, and be called back. So two men went forth to the Christian; and, concealing what had happened, they said to him, Lo, Daire is sick; may somewhat from thee be brought to him, if haply he may be healed. St. Patrick, however, knowing what had happened, said, Certainly. And he blessed some water, and gave it to them, saying, Go, sprinkle your horse with this water, and take him away with you. And they did so; and the horse came to life again, and they took him away with them; and Daire was healed by the sprinkling of the holy water.

And after these things Daire came to pay his respects to St. Patrick, bringing with him a wonderful bronze pot holding three gallons that had come from beyond the seas. And Daire said to the Saint, Lo, this bronze pot is for thee. And St. Patrick said *Grazacham*. And when Daire returned to his own house, he said, That is a stupid man, who said nothing more civil than *Grazacham* in return for a wonderful bronze three-gallon pot. And Daire then proceeded to say to his servants, Go, and bring us back our pot. So they went and said to Patrick, We are going to take away the pot. Nevertheless, St. Patrick, that time too said, *Grazacham*, Take it away. And they took it away. And Daire questioned his companions and said, What did the Christian say when ye took back the pot? And they answered, He just said *Grazacham*. Daire answered and said, *Grazacham*, when it is given! *Grazacham*, when it is taken away! his expression is so good that his pot must be brought back again to him with his *Grazacham*. And Daire came himself this time, and brought the pot to Patrick, saying, Thy pot must remain with thee; for thou art a steadfast and unchangeable man; moreover, as for that parcel of ground which thou didst once desire, I give it thee now, in so far as I possess it; and do thou dwell there.

And that is the city which is now called Ardd-Machæ.

And they went both of them out, St. Patrick and Daire, to inspect the admirable and acceptable gift that was being offered; and they ascended that high ground, and found a hind with her little fawn lying where now stands the altar of the Northern Church in Ardd-Machæ.

And St. Patrick's companions wanted to take the fawn and kill it; but the Saint did not wish this to be done, and would not allow it; nay, on the contrary, the Saint himself took the fawn and carried it on his shoulders. And the hind followed him, like a gentle and tame sheep until he let the fawn loose in another wood situated on the north side of Ardd-Machæ, where, to this very day, the learned say there are remaining certain signs of his power.

CHAPTER XXV

OF THE HEATHEN FOLK WORKING ON THE LORD'S DAY IN DEFIANCE OF PATRICK'S INSTRUCTIONS

Now on another occasion when St. Patrick was resting on the Lord's Day at the seaside, by the salt marsh which is on the northern shore, not very far away from the Hill of the Ox, he heard a loud noise of heathen folk working on the Lord's Day, making a rath. Patrick called them and forbad them to work on the Lord's Day. But they did not agree with what the Saint said; they even burst into laughter and mocked him. And St. Patrick said, *Mudebroth!* Although ye labour, it will not profit you. And this was fulfilled; for on the following night a mighty wind arose and stirred up the sea; and the storm destroyed the whole work of the heathen folk, according to the saying of the Saint.

CHAPTER XXVI

OF THE FRUITFUL LAND TURNED INTO A SALT MARSH AT PATRICK'S WORD

THE learned tell of a man who lived in the Plain of Inis, who was exceedingly harsh, and so grasping, and had run into such a pitch of folly and avarice, that one day when the booby saw the two oxen that drew St. Patrick's wagon resting and grazing, after their holy labours, in a meadow of his farm, the silly man violently and inconsiderately drove them off by force, in the very presence of St. Patrick.

And St. Patrick, enraged with him, cursed him and said, *Mudebrod!* thou hast done ill; this field of thine shall be of no profit to thee or to thy seed for ever; it shall be useless from this moment. And so it came to pass; for an overflowing inundation of the sea came on that very day, and flowed around and covered the whole field; and, as the prophet says, "A fruitful land was turned into a salt marsh for the wickedness of them that dwell therein." It is therefore sandy and barren from the day on which St. Patrick cursed it to the present time.

CHAPTER XXVII

OF THE DEATH OF MONEISEN, THE SAXON LADY

AND so I shall endeavour, if the Lord will, to narrate a few out of the many miracles performed by Patrick, bishop and eminent teacher of all Ireland, so to speak.

Once upon a time, when all Britain was numb with the chill of unbelief, there was a noble daughter of a certain king, and her name was Moneisen; and she was filled with the grace of the Holy Spirit. When some one sought her in marriage, she did not consent; and, though bathed in tears, she could not be forced against her will to adopt what was the lower life. For she was wont—amidst blows and floods of tears—to ask her mother and her nurse to tell her who was the Maker of the orb by which the whole world is lighted up; and she received an answer from which she ascertained that the Maker of the sun is He whose seat is the heaven.

When she was constantly urged to join herself to a husband in the bond of matrimony, she used—illuminated by the brightest light of the Holy Spirit—to say, I will on no account do this thing. For she sought through nature the Maker of the whole creation; following in this respect the example of the patriarch Abraham.

Her parents, having taken advice given to them by God, heard of Patrick as a man who was visited by the everlasting God every seventh day; and they sought the Scottic country with their daughter, looking for Patrick; and they found him after seeking for him with much toil. And he began to question them as if they were neophytes. Then the travellers began to cry aloud and say, We have had to come to thee, compelled on account of our daughter who is earnestly desirous to see God. Then he, filled with the Holy Ghost, raised his voice and said to her, Dost thou believe in God? And she said, I believe. Then he washed her with the sacred laver of the Spirit and water. And almost immediately afterwards, falling on the ground, she yielded up her spirit into the hands of the angels. She was buried where she died. Then Patrick prophesied that after twenty years her body would be reverently borne from that spot to a church hard by. And this afterwards came to pass; the relics of this maiden from beyond the seas are venerated there to this very day.

CHAPTER XXVIII

HOW ST. PATRICK SAW THE HEAVENS OPENED, AND THE SON OF GOD AND HIS ANGELS

THERE is a certain marvel wondrously wrought concerning the Christ-like and apostolic Patrick of whom we are speaking, which I shall unfold in a short narrative. As an experience of one still standing in the flesh, it is recorded only of him and of Stephen.

Once upon a time when he was going at night to a solitary place to pray, he gazed upon the familiar marvels of the heavens; and wishing to test his holy lad, who was most dear to him and trusty, he said, O my son, tell me, I pray thee, if thou perceivest the things which I perceive. Then the little boy, whose name was Benignus, said without hesitation, I know now the things which thou perceivest; for I see the heaven opened, and the Son of God and His angels. Then Patrick said, Now I perceive that thou art my worthy successor.

Immediately they reached with quickened step the accustomed place of prayer. These prayers were said in the middle of the bed of a river; and the little boy said, I cannot endure the chill of the water. For the water was too cold for him. Then Patrick told him to go down from a higher to a lower place. Nevertheless, he was able to keep his ground there for a long while; for he used to declare that he felt the water warm. Finally, not being able to stand long in that place, he climbed on to the land.

CHAPTER XXIX

OF THE CONFLICT OF ST. PATRICK WITH COROTICUS, KING OF AIL

I WILL not pass over in silence a certain wonderful deed of Patrick's. The vile action of a certain British king named Coroticus, a wretched cruel tyrant, was reported to him. Now this man was the greatest possible persecutor and slayer of Christians. Patrick, however, endeavoured by a letter to recall him to the way of truth; but he mocked at his salutary warnings. When, however, this was reported to Patrick, he prayed to the Lord and said, O God, if it be possible, banish this faithless man both from this world and the world to come.

No long time had elapsed when he caused a magical spell to be chanted before him, from which he heard that in a brief space he would pass away from the royal throne. And all the men dearest to him broke out into language of the same purport. He then, when he was in the midst of his court, took on the spot the form of a little fox—a pitiable object—and departed in the presence of his friends; and from that day and that hour, like flowing water that passeth away, he was never seen again.

These few particulars respecting the skill and the powers of St. Patrick did Muirchu-maccu-Machtheni draw up under the direction of Ædh, Bishop of the city of Slebte.

BOOK II

CHAPTER I

OF PATRICK'S DILIGENCE IN PRAYER

Every day "he used to sing all the psalms and hymns and the Apocalypse" of John and the spiritual songs of the Scriptures, whether he was at home or on a journey. Moreover he used to sign himself with the sign of the cross a hundred times every hour of the day and night. And whenever he saw a cross, he would alight from his car, and turn aside there to pray.

CHAPTER II

OF THE DEAD MAN WHO SPOKE TO HIM

So while journeying one day, he passed, without noticing it, a cross situate near the roadside. The driver, however, saw it; and when they had reached a certain inn which he had been making for, and they had begun prayers before dinner, the driver, I say, said, I saw a cross situate by the side of the road by which we came. On this, Patrick left the inn, and went back by the road by which he had come to the cross, and prayed there. And he saw there a sepulchre, and a dead man buried in that tomb. And he asked him by what death he had died, and in what faith he had lived. And the dead man replied, I was a heathen in my life, and I was buried here.

Now there was a certain woman dwelling in another province whose son, who had long been parted from her, died, and was buried while he was away from her. But after some days, the grieving mother bewailed her lost son, and mistakenly thinking the sepulchre of the heathen man to be the tomb of her son, she erected the cross beside the heathen man.

And this was the reason, Patrick said, why he had not seen the cross, because it was a heathen burial-place. And a greater miracle thence resulted, to wit, that a dead man should speak, and that he who had died in the faith of Christ should be discovered, and that the merit of the fostering cross should be put by him, when the sign [*i. e.* the cross] was placed on the right site.

CHAPTER III

OF THE SUNDAY NIGHT THAT WAS LIGHTED UP, SO THAT THE HORSES WERE FOUND

Now, it was Patrick's custom not to walk abroad from the eve of the Lord's Day at night [*i. e.* Saturday evening] till the morning of the second day of the week. Accordingly, on a certain Lord's Day, when spending the night in the open country, as a mark of respect for the holy season, heavy rain came on with a violent wind. But though the whole country was ruined by the heavy rain, yet in the place in which the holy bishop was passing the night it was as dry as Gideon's bowl and fleece.

The driver then came up, and told how the horses had been lost; he bewailed them as if they had been his dear friends; and he could not go to look for them, as the darkness prevented him seeing them. So the kindly feelings of Patrick, the kind father, were roused, and he said to the weeping driver, God, who is a ready " helper in distress, in times-of trouble," will afford His help, and thou shalt find the horses for which thou weepest. And on this, stretching his bare hand out of his sleeve, he raised it aloft; and his five fingers, like luminaries, lighted up the adjacent country. And by the light of the outstretched hand the driver found the horses he had lost, and an end was put to his moans. But the driver, [Patrick's] companion, did not publish this miracle until Patrick's death.

CHAPTER IV

OF HOW THE ANGEL FORBAD HIM TO DIE IN MICHI [MACHI]

BUT after such miracles, which have been recorded elsewhere, and which the world celebrates with faithful lips, as the day of his death drew near, an angel came to him, and spoke to him concerning his death. Accordingly, he sent to Ardd-Machæ, which he loved beyond all other places. So he ordered that many men should come to him, to bring him whither he wished to go.

CHAPTER V

OF THE BURNING BUSH IN WHICH THE ANGEL WAS

THEN, of his own accord, he took his journey with his companions to Machi, the land much desired. But by the way-side a certain bush burned with fire and was not consumed, as formerly happened to Moses in the bush.

Now Victor was the angel who was wont often to visit Patrick ; and Victor sent another angel to forbid Patrick to go whither he desired to go. And he said to him, Wherefore dost thou set out without the advice of Victor? Therefore Victor calleth thee, and do thou turn aside to him. And he turned aside as he was bidden, and asked what he ought to do. And the angel answered and said, Return unto the place whence thou camest, that is, to Sabul ; and the four petitions which thou didst desire are granted thee.

CHAPTER VI

OF THE FOUR PETITIONS OF PATRICK

THE first petition : that thy jurisdiction be in Ardd-Machæ.

The second petition : that whoever, on the day of his death, shall sing the hymn composed concerning thee, thou shalt be the judge of his repentance of his sins.

The third petition : that the descendants of Dichu, who received thee kindly, shall receive mercy, and not perish.

The fourth petition : that all the Irish shall be judged by thee in the Day of Judgement, as it was said to the Apostles, "And ye shall sit and judge the twelve tribes of Israel"; that thou mayest be the judge of those to whom thou wast an apostle.

CHAPTER VII

OF THE DAY OF HIS DEATH, AND OF THE TIME OF HIS LIFE, 120 YEARS

RETURN, therefore, as I bid thee ; and when thou diest, thou shalt go the way of thy fathers. (And this took place on the 17th day of March, when the 120 years of his whole life had been completed, as it is celebrated in all parts of Ireland.)

CHAPTER VIII

OF THE BOUNDARY SET TO THE NIGHT, AND OF THE DARKNESS OF TWELVE NIGHTS TAKEN AWAY

AND thou shalt set a boundary against the night. Because on the day of his death there was no night ; and in the province in which his funeral was conducted, for twelve days "night did not come down and wrap the earth with dusky wings," and "the gloom of the night was not so great, and Hesperus did not bring on the shadows that shew stars." And the people of Ulaid said that to the very end of the year in which he died the nights were never so dark as formerly they had been. And this, no doubt, took place to shew forth the worthiness of so great a man.

Now if any one would faithlessly deny that a boundary was set against the night, so that night was not seen throughout the whole province for the short space of time in which the mourning for Patrick was conducted, let him hear and mark carefully how a token of recovery was shewn on the dial of Ahaz to Hezekiah when he was sick, and so forth.

CHAPTER IX

[OF THE SACRIFICE RECEIVED AT THE HANDS OF BISHOP TASSACH]

Now when the hour of his death drew nigh, he received the Sacrifice from Bishop Tassach, as the *viaticum* of a blessed life, as Victor the angel told him.

CHAPTER X

OF THE WATCH KEPT BY THE ANGELS BY THE BODY OF PATRICK ON THE FIRST NIGHT

On the first night of his funeral, the angels kept watch over the holy body in the customary manner of vigils and psalms, while all those were sleeping who had come to watch on that first night. But on the other nights men guarded the body, praying and singing psalms. Now after the angels had gone away into heaven, they left behind them a most sweet odour as of honey and a delicious fragrance as of wine, that it might be fulfilled which was spoken in the blessing of the patriarch Jacob, "See, the smell of my son is as the smell of a field which the Lord hath blessed"

CHAPTER XI

OF THE ADVICE GIVEN BY THE ANGEL
CONCERNING HIS BURIAL

Now when the angel came to him, he gave him advice as to the manner of his burial :—Let two unbroken oxen be chosen, and let them go whithersoever they will, and in whatever place they lie down, let a church be built in honour of thy poor body.

And as the angel said, restive bullocks were chosen, and they draw a wagon, with a litter firmly fixed on it in which the holy body was, yoked to their shoulders. And oxen from the herds of Conail, from the place that is called Clocher, on the east of Findubair, were made glorious by being chosen for this purpose. And they went forth, the will of God guiding them, to Dun-Lethglaisse, where Patrick was buried.

CHAPTER XII

OF THE FIRE THAT BURST FORTH FROM HIS TOMB

And he said to him, Let no relics of thy body be taken from the ground, and let a cubit's depth of earth be over thy body. And it was proved in recent times that this was done by the command of God. Because, when a church was built over his body, the men who were digging the ground saw fire bursting from his tomb ; and ran away in alarm at the flame-bearing fire of flame.

CHAPTER XIII

OF THE LOUGH WHICH ROSE, THAT THERE MIGHT
NOT BE WAR CONCERNING HIS BODY

At the time of his death, a sore contention, amounting even to war, arose concerning the relics of St. Patrick, between the Ui-Neill and the men of Airthir on one side,

H

and the men of Ulaid on the other; that is, between those who had once been neighbours and kinsmen, but were now bitter enemies. The contest, fed by their anger, took place by the channel which is called the Hill of the Ox.

By the merit of Patrick and by the mercy of God, to prevent the shedding of blood, the sea swelled up with high and curling billows; and the tops of the waves split the vault of heaven; and the ridges quivering on the billows rushed to battle, sometimes with quavering laughter, and sometimes with tawny valleys, as if to restrain the enmity of terrible nations; for such the peoples are. The wildness of the lough arose, and forbad the people to fight.

CHAPTER XIV

OF THE FORTUNATE DELUSION OF THE PEOPLES

Now after Patrick had been buried, and the swelling of the lough had been assuaged, the men of Airthir arose again, and the Ui-Neill rush fiercely to battle against the men of Ulaid. And thoroughly prepared and armed for war, they burst forth at the place where the blessed body lay.

But they were misled by a fortunate delusion. Supposing that they had found the two oxen and the wagon, they thought they were carrying off the holy body. And with the body and such armed preparation, they got as far as the river Cabcenne; and at that point the body was not present with them.

For it was impossible that there should be peace concerning a body so august and blessed, unless, by the will of God, a vision shewn opportunely should be seen in such wise Lest that which had been the salvation of countless souls should be turned to destruction and death, it [the body] was displayed by a fortunate delusion; just as, once upon a time, the Syrians, blinded that they might not slay the holy prophet Elisha, were, through Divine providence, led by Elisha to Samaria. So this delusion was brought about to bring peace to the peoples.

CHAPTER XV

OF THE WEEKLY MEETINGS [OF THE ANGEL] WITH PATRICK

To revert to the subject of prayer :—

The angel was wont to come to him on every seventh day of the week; and, as one man talks with another, so Patrick enjoyed the angel's conversation.

Moreover in the sixteenth year of his age he was taken captive, and for six years he was a slave, and throughout thirty changes of service the angel used to come to him; and he enjoyed angelical counsel and conversation.

Before he went from Scotia to the Latins, he used to pray a hundred times in the day and a hundred times in the night.

One time, when minding his swine, he lost them; and the angel came to him and shewed him where the swine were. Another time, moreover, when the angel was saying many things to him, after he had finished speaking, he placed one foot upon a rock in Scirit [and the other] on Mount Mis, and ascended to heaven in his sight. And the footmarks of the angel can be seen remaining on the rock to this very day. And in that place he spoke to him thirty times; and that place is a place of prayer, and there the prayers of the faithful obtain the happiest fruit.

NOTES ON THE CONFESSION

C. 1. *Patrick.* His full name, in Roman style, was probably Patricius Magonus Sucatus (Bury, *St. Patrick*, p. 23). The fourth name, Cothirthiacus, added by Tirechán, is simply a Latinization of Cothraige, or Coithrige, which is the Irish form of Patrick (see Bury, *St. Patrick*, pp. 268, 291) An earlier form is Qatrige, Quadriga. This suggested a derivation from *quattuor* "Many were they whom he served, Cothraige (servant) of a fourfold household" (Hymn *Genair Patraicc*); "Cothirthiacus, because he was a slave in the houses of four magicians" (Tirechán). The name Magonus is attested by Tirechán. Sucat (Hymn *Genair Patraicc*) seems to have been the name by which he was familiarly known in his own home, "his name from his parents" (*Vit Trip*, i. 17). A note on the Hymn, quoted *Vit. Trip*, ii. 413, explains Sucat as *Deus Belli, uel, Fortis belli.* It is spelt Sochet by Muirchu, and Succetus by Tirechán.

"*Patrick the sinner*" recurs in Conf. 62, Letter 1. *Peccator* is a self-depreciatory epithet, almost conventional ; cf. Dionysius Exiguus.

Illiterate. It is difficult to find an English equivalent for *rusticus* (here, and c. 12) and *rusticitas* (46), which will combine the meaning "illiterate" with a suggestion of the primary signification, "rural, rustic." St. Patrick plays upon the double meaning in c. 11, where he quotes Ecclus. vii. 16 ("And husbandry (*rusticatio*) was ordained by the Most High"), as a divine intimation that illiteracy is not a fatal disqualification in a bishop.

Calpurnius. Calpornus is the spelling in A, Calpornius or Calpurnius is found in the other MSS., Cualfarnus in Muirchu. He belonged socially to the class of *decuriones* (see note on Letter, 10).

Muirchu repeats, without comment, the account here given of the ecclesiastical standing of Calpurnius and Potitus. But Marianus Scotus, in his Chronicle *s a.* 394, and *Vit. Trip.*, i. 9, make Calpurnius a presbyter and Potitus a deacon ; so also the Preface B to the Hymn of St. Sechnall On the other hand, the Hymn *Genair Patraicc* suppresses the clerical status of the father and grandfather : "Son of Calpurn, son of Potid, grandson of deacon Odisse." The reading here of R, *Calpurnium diaconum quondam* is possibly intended to suggest that Calpurnius had ceased to be a deacon before his marriage. Jocelin (*Vita* vi. 1), on the other hand, represents his ordination as having taken place after the birth of his children.

There is, however, nothing surprising in St. Patrick's statement. The general practice of the primitive Church, still continued in the East, permitted the secular clergy—presbyters and deacons—to marry before their ordination, and this was the custom at Milan until the eleventh century. The Council of Trullo, 692, enforced celibacy, or at least continence, on bishops. In the West, the Council of Elvira in Spain, A.D. 305, tried to enforce celibacy on all men in Holy Orders; but there is plenty of evidence that the standard of strictness varied very much in different countries. Rules which were with difficulty enforced in Spain might well be relaxed, or non-existent, in Britain.

The name of St. Patrick's great-grandfather, Odissus, is inserted here in the margin of A.

The name of Patrick's mother was Concessa (so Muirchu; *Vita* iv. 1, etc.). Marianus Scotus adds that she was a sister of St. Martin of Tours, "a kinswoman of Martin's" (*Vit. Trip.*, 1. 9). "Lupait and Tigris were his two sisters" (Preface B to Hymn of St. Sechnall).

Banavem Taberniæ. The first part of this name is spelt Bannavem in A and Muirchu (B). The second half is Taburniæ in P, and Thaburinde in Muirchu.

The first point on which we can be certain about Patrick's birth-place is that it was in Great Britain. See c. 23, "And again, after a few years, I was in Britain with my kindred"; and c. 43, "Proceeding to Britain . . . as to my fatherland and kindred." Muirchu says emphatically that Patrick "was of the British race and born in Britain."

As to the name of his native place, Prof. Bury (*St Patrick*, p 323), says, "that Bannaventa is the name there can, I think, be no doubt." No satisfactory explanation, however, has been given of the ending *berniæ* or *burniæ*, or *burinde*. The suggestion that it is a contraction for *Britanniæ* is inadmissible. Patrick always speaks of *Britanniæ*, not *Britannia*. I cannot help thinking that Lanigan was right in supposing that Banavem (or Bonaven, as he spells it) might represent a Celtic place-name, *river's mouth* (Todd, *St. Patrick*, p. 357); and that *taberniæ* is connected with *taberna*, a tavern. It is not a fatal objection to this theory that it is inconceivable that a Celtic town should have only one *taberna* in it.

In what part of Great Britain was this town? Muirchu supplies one clear piece of evidence: it was "not far distant from our sea," *i. e.* the Irish Channel. This seems fatal to the claims for Daventry, in Northamptonshire. He adds, "We have ascertained repeatedly that this place is unquestionably Ventre." Probus, however, read in his copy of Muirchu, *Nentriæ provinciæ* for *Ventre*. These variants *Ventre* and *Nentriæ* are not very remote in appearance from *Nemthur*, which is the name as given in the Hymn *Genair Patraicc* · "Patrick was born in Nemthur; this is what is related in stories" An ancient note on this line identifies Nemthur with Alcluith or Ail-Cluade, the Rock of Clyde, *i. e.* Dumbarton on the Clyde; and with this agrees the Preface (B) to the Hymn of St. Sechnall, "As to Patrick, his origin was of the Britons of Her-cluaide.

Coroticus was the ruler of Alcluith; and in the Letter (c. 2) Patrick speaks of the soldiers of Coroticus as his fellow-citizens (cf. c 11, "My own know me not"). This point cannot be pressed (see note *in loc.*), but the expression is at least not unfavourable to the identification of

Patrick's birth-place with Dumbarton or some place in the neighbour-hood (Killpatrick, see reff. in Hogan's ed. of Muirchu).   On the other hand, Prof. Bury, while maintaining that Coroticus "represented th · Roman defence of North Britain" (*op. cit.*, p. 314), thinks it unlikely that the Roman civil organization, implied in the title *decurio*, had reached so far north; and he places "Bannaventa" "perhaps in the regions of the lower Severn" (*op. cit*, p. 17).   In his Preface, he states on the authority of Prof. Rhys, that there are three places named Banwen in Glamorganshire.   The "South Wales" theory, however, would never have been heard of had not Coroticus been identified with "Caredig, who, in the fifth century, held and gave his name (still sur-viving in *Cardigan*) to that region" (Gwynn, *Book of Armagh*, p xc);   and then the language of the Letter, quoted above, was supposed to prove that Patrick and Coroticus belonged to the same district.   Prof Bury (*op. cit.*, p. 315) thinks the view which identifies Coroticus with Caredig as now hardly worth mentioning.   This is not the only case in historical criticism in which a superstructure appears an attractive residence after the foundations of it have been dug up.   In view of the fact that the evidence as to the condition of Strathclyde in the fifth century is obscure and conflicting, I am still disposed to think that the case against Dumbarton is not proven.

I knew not the true God.   The "marvellous light" which accom-panies and follows conversion always makes the time before it seem darkness.   It would be unreasonable to accept literally Patrick's self-depreciatory statements made here and elsewhere.   If the seed of eternal life had not been already sown in him, servitude in a heathen land could not have produced in him the flower of holiness.   The prayers which he repeated in the land of his captivity so fervently, and with an ever deepening sense of their meaning, must have been learnt at home;   and it is probable that he had begun the rudiments of other learning as well in his father's house;   for his language in c. 10 ("My sins prevented me from mastering what I had read through before") seems to imply that his education had been interrupted by his captivity.

To Ireland, "Hiberione."   The form *Hiberio* is also found in Conf. 16, 23, 28, 41, 62; Letter 1, 5, 10, 12.   The form *Hiberia* occurs in Letter 16   *The Irish* are *Hiberionaces*, Conf. 23; *Hibernæ gentes*, 37.

C. 4.   The wording of this creed passage is borrowed unmistakably from the Commentary on the Apocalypse by Victorinus of Pettau in Upper Pannonia, who was martyred in the Diocletian persecution (see Bigne, *Bibl. Vet. Patr.* iii., p. 418 c).   Patrick's dependence on this now little-known author was demonstrated in 1894 by Kattenbusch in *Das Apostolische Symbol* ii , p. 212 f.   See also a review by Hauss-sleiter in *Gottingische gelehrte Anzeige* for 1898.   For this information, which I have verified, I am indebted to Mr. M Esposito's note in the *Journal of Theological Studies*, July, 1918.   Dr. F. R. Montgomery Hitchcock has noted some less striking parallels between this chapter and the teaching of Irenæus (*Hermathena* xiv., 1907, pp. 168 ff.).

C. 9   St. Patrick means that his Latin style—at no time, probably, very polished—had been rendered more uncouth by his long residence in Ireland and use of the Irish language, "a tongue not my own." Cf. c. 1, "Men of another nation."

C. 10 *For as the spirit yearns*, etc. The meaning of this obscure sentence seems to be that, though the Divine Spirit, working on the human disposition, causes it to display the soul and understanding of a man, it displays the soul, etc., as it actually is; no amount of piety will make Patrick appear other than illiterate and unable to express himself.

C. 11. *Not a few*. The unnamed opponents who are mentioned again in cc. 26, 37.

C. 13. *Clever sirs*. This is Prof. Bury's rendering, *domini cati*. However, *dominicati* (one word) might be "lordly," as I rendered it in my first ed.

C. 14. *The rule of faith*. The phrase *mensura fidei* (Rom. xii. 3) is used by Victorinus of Pettau, from whom Patrick took it, in the sense of *regula fidei*.

Many thousands of persons. The same claim is made in identical terms in c. 50. Cf. c. 42, and Letter, cc. 2, 12, 16.

C. 16. *Flocks*, "pecora" The word connotes sheep rather than pigs; but Tirechán (fol. 9, r° *b*) says that Miliuc "porcarium possuit eum"; and similarly Muirchu (ii. 15) tells how when Patrick was "minding his swine," the angel helped him to find them when they were lost.

C 17. *Thy ship is ready*. Tirechán adds, *Rise and walk*. Tirechán says that Patrick served Miliuc for seven years.

The man, i. e Miliucc (Muirchu); Miliuc-maccu-Boin (Tirechán).

Prospered my way for good, "qui viam meam ad bonum dirigebat." The Bollandist ed., following the Tripartite Life (i 22), takes *bonum* here as a place-name, *i. e.* Boandum, the river Boyne. There is no specification in the other *Lives* of the place where Patrick embarked.

C. 18. *I had to sail*. "ut haberem navigare." This is an example of the use of *habeo* found in Low Latin to express the future tense, *e.g.* in the Athanasian Creed, *resurgere habent* = "will rise again." Dr. F. R. Montgomery Hitchcock quotes two instances of this use of *habere* from Irenæus (*Irenæus of Lugdunum*, p. 353). On the other hand, Probus (*Vita* v 4) took *haberem* here in the usual sense, referring it to the passage-money, and interpolated *non* into the text. Probus attributes the wroth of the ship-master to the fact that Patrick admitted that he had not wherewith to pay the fare.

Suck their breasts. The context seems to imply that this indicates the sailors' method of "making friends," some heathenish custom with which Patrick refused to comply "because of the fear of God." Prof. Bury, in a note kindly communicated to me, says, "I take *sugere mammellas* to be an interesting piece of evidence for a primitive ceremony of adoption. It is the custom among some peoples, in adopting children, to go through the form of a mock birth (see J. G. Frazer, *Golden Bough*, ed. 2, i. 21). In some cases, the child to be adopted is placed under the gown or dress of the adoptive mother, and has to creep out —a make-believe birth The existence of such ceremonies justifies us in supposing that the phrase *sugere mammellas* arose out of a make-

believe suckling, and meant 'to be adopted by' . . . It may mean no
more than 'I refused to enter into a close intimacy with them.'"

C. 19. *We reached land.* Gaul; not Britain, as Muirchu (i. 1) says.
Muirchu expected the divine promise of c. 17 to be fulfilled at once,
and misunderstood c. 23, "And again, after a few years, I was in
Britain" Patrick had not been in Britain since his captivity. See
next note.

Their dogs. The cargo of the ship was of dogs. Prof. Bury (*St.
Patrick*, p. 341) notes that "Celtic hounds were highly valued in the
south [of Europe]. . . . Mr. Olden (*History of the Church of Ireland*,
pp. 16, 18) acutely suggests that Patrick, so long the servant of an Irish
chieftain, had become skilled in the management of wolf-hounds, and
that this consideration may have determined the traders to take him on
board. . . . The cargo of dogs seems to support the conclusion that
it was to Gaul, not to Britain, that the traders sailed. They might have
landed at either Nantes or Bordeaux." That it was Bordeaux is
indicated by Probus (Brotgalum, *i.e* Boitgalum, from the Irish
Bordgal).

Thanks be to God. Deo gratias was a favourite expression of St.
Patrick's; it occurs twice in the *Dicta Patricii*, and in Conf 19, 23, 42;
Letter 17. *Gratias* or *gratiam ago* occurs in cc. 30, 34, 46. See also
the story told by Muirchu (i. 24) about Patrick's reiterated *grazacham*,
i e. *gratias agamus.* Muirchu and *Vita* iii (16) say that Patrick on
this occasion abstained from all the food, not merely from the honey.

C 20 *And he fell upon me.* I have adopted Mr. M. Esposito's
correction of my former rendering, "And there fell upon me"

Helias. By the time that Patrick came to write his account of this
nightmare, he had learnt that Helios was a [Greek] name for the sun;
and the coincidence of his shouting *Helias* with the rising of the sun
seemed due to a divine suggestion to his ignorant mind of a supposed
connexion between the two words. The same contrast between Christ,
the true sun, and the sun in the heavens, is found in c. 60 So Probus,
"Cum trina voce invocasset Christum solem verum." On the other
hand, *Helias* can only mean *Elijah;* and Muirchu and the other ancient
Lives, with the exception of Probus, state that Patrick invoked this
Old Testament Saint. Sun worship was so prevalent in Europe at this
time, that possibly the Greek name for the sun would be known to
persons who had even less Greek than had Patrick.

C. 21. This second captivity refers to the period during which
Patrick was with the traders after they landed in France. The "many
years" are the six years that had elapsed since the Irish pirates tore
him from his home. The appearance of the swine seems to have
occurred on the twenty-eighth day after the landing; and Patrick was
with the sailors, from the day they left Ireland, for ninety-three days
in all. Prof Bury (*St. Patrick*, p 294) "believes that the sentence
is a parenthetical reference to his lifework in Ireland, considered as a
second captivity." This explanation seems far fetched.

C. 22. *Dry quarters* possibly, "dry weather."

C 23. The "few years" that elapsed between his escape from the
traders and his return to Britain were probably spent at Lérins.

Muirchu (i. 5) states that Patrick was now thirty years of age (see note). This is probably a precarious inference from c. 27.

In Britain: "in Britanniis." The plural form *Britanniæ*, which St. Patrick always uses (see cc. 32, 43), has reference to the provinces into which the country was divided by the Romans, viz Britannia Prima, Britannia Secunda, Maxima Cæesariensis, Flavia Cæsariensis and Valentia.

Victoricus, in all likelihood, was one of Patrick's Gallic friends with whom he may have discussed projects of missionary work in Ireland. He was transformed in later years into Patrick's guardian angel (see Muirchu i. 1, 7 ; ii. 5, 15 ; Tirechán, *passim*).

The Wood of Foclut, Foclut. The Wood of Fochlad or Fochlath included the townlands of Crosspatrick and Donaghmore in the parish of Killala, in the barony of Tirawley, Co Mayo. According to Prof. Bury (*St Patrick*, p. 335), the wood was not confined to north-western Mayo, but extended southward to Murrisk.

The words which St. Patrick heard were amplified in later times. Tirechán (fol. 11 r° *a*) says, "He heard the voices of children crying with great outcry in the wombs of their mothers, and saying, Come, holy Patrick, to save us (Veni, sancte Patrici, salvos nos facere) This is the version of the words as given in the third antiphon appended to the Hymn of St. Sechnall. On the other hand, Muirchu (i. 7) represents the angel Victoricus as saying, "The boys and girls of the Wood of Fochlath are calling thee."

In my first edition of the *Libri S. Patricii*, I rendered the words, "We beseech thee, holy youth, to come *hither* and walk among us." Dr. Gwynn, whom I consulted on the point, was so convinced that the scene of Patrick's captivity was in Co. Antrim, not in Co. Mayo, that he thought *et adhuc* might be taken as a careless writing of *adhuc et.* This may have been the reading in Muirchu's copy of the Confession ; for the title of chapter 7 of Book i. of his Life has *ut veniret adhuc.* In Dr. Gwynn's edition of the Book of Armagh, p lxxxiii. he renders it *moreover.* On the other hand, in Conf. 21 it means *once more.* See Dr. Gwynn's note, *op. cit.,* p. cclxxxix. f.

C. 26. *Assailed,* "temptauit." Patrick uses *tempto* rather in the sense of *assail* than of *induce to sin.* So in c. 20, Satan "tempted" him by throwing huge rocks on him. This attack seems to have been made after Patrick had laboured some time in Ireland as bishop. It may have been on his visit to Rome, when he was "approved in the Catholic faith" (Ann Ult *sub. an.* 441). See Bury, *op. cit.,* p. 367. But see Introd. p. 17

C. 27. The thirty years had elapsed since the fault—whatever it was —had been committed. Patrick may mean that thirty years had passed since the confession of the fault ; but this does not seem so probable.

Against me. "me adversus." The transposition of prepositions is a common characteristic of Low Latin. See Krusch, *Ionæ Vitæ Sanctorum,* p. 58.

C. 29. *The aforesaid persons·* i. e. those to whom St. Patrick refers in c. 26, "not a few of my elders."

C. 29. *A writing void of honour over against my face;* "Scriptum erat contra faciem meam sine honore ". *Contra* here means *over against*, as in Dan. v. 5 (a passage which Patrick possibly had in his mind), "The fingers . . . wrote over against the candlestick," "Manus hominis scribentis contra candelabrum." A characteristic feature of St. Patrick's visions was, that in them his own body is not that which sees, but is itself one of the things seen.

The key to the understanding of this vision, and to the translation of the description of it, must be sought in the whole context. The opening words of c. 32 prove that the divine utterance in this chapter was directed against Patrick's false friend; and c. 30 indicates that it involved a vindication of Patrick's character. But Patrick is satisfied with the divine approval of himself; and, consistently with his practice of "naming no names," he will not be betrayed here into a disclosure which would cause bitterness to others. If we suppose, by way of illustration, his false friend's name to have been Germanus, what Patrick heard was, "We have seen with anger the face of Germanus." Germanus is "the person designated" in c 27 as "My dearest friend." In the "answer of God" his name was expressed, "laid bare," *nudato nomine.* The attack in writing over against Patrick's face was more than counterbalanced by the wrathful regard of God against the face of his friend. This explanation seems more satisfactory than that of Dr. Gwynn (*op. cit.*, p. lxxxv.), who takes *designati* as nom. pl. rather than gen. sing., and *nudato nomine* and *sine honore* as mutually explanatory:— "He saw his own face, with a writing set against it, in which his episcopal style was withheld from him." This is quite likely. But Dr. Gwynn's rendering of the words heard is rather unnatural : "We have seen the face with displeasure; [we who have been] designated by name stript [of the title of Bishop]."

C. 32. *That contention ·* "dissensionem." An allusion to Acts xv. 39, the sharp contention between two friends, Paul and Barnabas. But the other reading, *defensionem*, might be an echo of 2 Tim. iv. 16, "At my first defence no one took my part." The rest of the verse has been quoted by Patrick at the end of c. 26.

C. 33. *If man had said this.* "This" refers to "the answer of God," *cf.* cc. 29, 32. "Man" is emphatic : If it were merely man, and not God, that thus rebuked my old friend, I should not have disclosed the fact at all.

C. 34. *Offer . . . a living victim.* This verse (Rom. xii. 1) is also quoted in the Hymn of St. Sechnall, x., "Quam [carnem] ut hostiam placentem uivam offert Domino."

The limit beyond which no man dwells, "usque ubi nemo ultra est." Cf. c. 51, "usque ad exteras partes ubi nemo ultra erat." When Patrick looked westward from Croaghpatrick he little dreamt that there were men beyond the Atlantic Ocean.

C. 35. *Unlearned:* "idiotam." This emendation of the meaningless *ideo tamen* of the MSS. implies a reference to Acts iv. 13, "homines sine litteris et idiotæ."

C. 37. *My free condition.* "ingenuitatem meam." Cf. Letter, 10, "Ingenuus fui secundum carnem" . . . uendidi . . . nobilitatem meam.

C. 38. *Confirmed* "consummarentur." This verb *consummare* is also used of the rite of Confirmation in c. 51. But in Letter, 2, the word is *confirmare*, which may be an indication that the Letter was written at a later date than the Confession.

C. 40. *We ought to fish . . . spread our nets.* This passage may have been in St. Sechnall's mind when he wrote (iv.):

> "Dominus illum elegit ut doceret barbaras
> Nationes ut piscaret per doctrinæ retia "

Muirchu, though familiar with the Confession, is probably thinking of the hymn, when he says (i. 7), "Victoricus . . . visited him . . . saying that the time had arrived for him to go, and with the Gospel *net fish for* the wild and *savage tribes* to whom the Lord had sent him *to teach them.*"

C. 41. The words *Filii Scottorum et filiæ regulorum monachi et virgines Christi* occur again in Letter, 12.

C. 42. *One blessed lady.* The incident to which reference is here made reminds us of other conversions of young women of noble birth in the ministry of St. Patrick. The story of the death of Moneisen, the Saxon lady, in Muirchu (i. 27), and that of Ethne and Fedelm, daughters of King Loigaire, in Tirechán (fol. 12, rº.), have in common the feature of death following what we should call a hasty baptism. The language used here suggests that this *benedicta Scotta* was no longer alive when Patrick wrote.

She seized on that, etc.: "arripuit illud." This apparently refers to the vow of perpetual virginity. Cf. Matt. xi. 12, "Regnum cælorum uim patitur : et uiolenti rapiunt illud," where the O.L. has *diripiunt* for *rapiunt.*

This *benedicta Scotta* may perhaps be identified with Cinnu or Cymnia, daughter of Echaid or Echu, son of Crimthan. Her father had desired that she should marry the son of Cormac, son of Coirbre, son of Niall; but allowed her to take the veil. Patrick entrusted her to Cechtumbar, abbess of Druimm-Dubain (*Vit. Trip*, i. 177).

Our race. People of British origin, but born in Ireland. Patrick here speaks as if he were writing in Britain for Britons.

C. 43 *As far as Gaul.* These words, expressing the utmost limits of Patrick's longings, seem to imply that his travels on the Continent had not extended further than Gaul. Even if he had visited Italy, Gaul was his spiritual home

C. 44. *Chastity.* Cf. Hymn of St. Sechnall, x., "Kastam qui custodit carnem ob amorem Domini "

I have not led a perfect life. Ctr. Hymn of St. Sechnall, i., "Perfectamque propter vitam æquatur apostolis."

C. 50. *A scruple:* "scriptula" = scriptulum = *scrupulum,* the twenty-fourth part of an ounce, the smallest division of anything; possibly here used of the *screpal* or *sical,* an ancient Celtic silver coin weighing twenty-four grains (Joyce, *Social History of Ancient Ireland,* ii., p. 381).

C. 53. *I paid to those who were judges.* For *iudicabant,* the cognate MSS. CF₃F₄ read *indicabant,* "those who shewed the way." Tirechán (fol. 10 vº b) fixes this incident as taking place on Patrick's journey to the Wood of Fochlath in the company of Endeus and his brothers: "Patrick moreover expended the value of fifteen souls of men [slaves], as he states in his writing, of silver and of gold, that no action of bad men should hinder them on their right road as they traversed the whole of Ireland" Patrick was eager to reach his goal as quickly as possible, to keep Easter at the Wood of Fochlath The local authorities had it in their power to delay his progress; it was not a question of getting guides, but facilities.

C. 56 *Chose me.* "elegit me." There is a reference here and in Letter, 6, to John xv 16, 19, "Ego elegi vos." St. Sechnall's Hymn (iv.), says of Patrick, "Dominus illum elegit ut doceret barbaras nationes," etc.

C. 58 *Bear to him faithful witness* "Reddam testimonium fidele." The reading [*me*] *testem fidelem* is supported by the Hymn of St. Sechnall, xix., "Testis Domini fidelis in lege catholica"; but it involves an unnatural use of *reddere*

C. 60. The contrast emphasised in this chapter and in c 20, between the material sun and Christ, the true sun, is a polemical thrust at the worship of Mithra, the Persian sun-god, whose cult was popular all over the Roman Empire during the first four or five centuries of our era.

NOTES ON THE LETTER

C. 1. "*Patrick the sinner, unlearned verily,*" is one of the Saint's recurrent phrases ; it occurs also in Conf. 62.

Appointed by God. Cf. Hymn of St. Sechnall, iii., "Cujusque apostolatum a Deo sortitus est."

Not regarded . . . my life. Cf. Hymn of St. Sechnall, xv., "Pio qua [plebe] ad Christi exemplum tradidit animam."

C. 2. *My fellow-citizen.* This expression cannot be pressed so as to make it a certain proof that Patrick's native place was Alcluith (Dumbarton), the headquarters of Coroticus. "Coroticus and his milites represented the Roman defence of North Britain" (Bury, *op. cit.*, p. 314). They were, then, citizens of the Roman Empire, as Patrick was ; but they were, in his opinion, unworthy of the honour (see Introd., p. 15).

They are dead while they live. Cf. 1 Tim. v. 6, "Vivens mortua est."

Apostate Picts. The epithet *apostate* is applied again, in c. 15, to the Picts. St. Ninian of Whitherne had converted the Southern Picts some time between A.D. 394 and 432.

C. 3. *A holy presbyter.* Possibly Benignus, as Ware conjectured.

C. 4. *Devil . . . ensnared.* An allusion to "the snare of the devil," 1 Tim. iii. 7 ; vi. 9.

C. 10. *A decurion.* A *decurio*, or *curialis*, was a member of the *curia* of a town under the Roman Empire. "The *curia* of a town consisted of a certain number of the richest landowners who were responsible to the treasury for a definite sum, which it was their business to collect from all the proprietors in the district" (Bury, *History of the Later Roman Empire*, i. p. 27). Gibbon in his remarks on the Theodosian code, which was promulgated in A.D. 438, says: "The laborious offices, which could be productive only of envy and reproach, of expense and danger, were imposed on the *decurions*, who formed the corporations of the cities, and whom the severity of the Imperial laws had condemned to sustain the burthens of civil society" (*Decline and Fall,* ed. Bury, ii. p. 192.

C. 13. *Eve did not understand.* Cf. "Greedily she ingorg'd without restraint, And knew not eating death" (*Paradise Lost*, ix. 791).

C. 14. *Roman Gauls* (see Introd., p. 15). The insertion of *Christianorum* after *Gallorum* in the later MSS. is superfluous ; the natives of that part of Gaul which lay within the Roman Empire were, in Patrick's thought of them, Christians.

The Franks and other heathen. The Franks were converted *en masse* to Christianity, with Clovis their king, in A.D. 496.

C. 17. " *Ye departed from the world to Paradise,*" is given as one of the Sayings of Patrick in the Book of Armagh (fol. 9 r° *a*).

C. 18. *Ye . . . shall reign with apostles.* In St. Sechnall's Hymn, xxiii., it is said of Patrick himself, "Cum apostolis regnabit sanctus super Israel." See note on Muirchu, ii. 6.

C. 21. *Peace . . . to the Father*, etc. The letter of a bishop might naturally end with the words, *Pax vobiscum.* But conventional forms of politeness are out of place in a missive which is a denunciation of an enemy of Christ. The only persons in the immediate vicinity of Coroticus with whom St. Patrick was at peace were the Father and the Son and the Holy Ghost ; so he sends to Them his greeting of peace in the form of a doxology.

NOTES ON MUIRCHU'S "LIFE OF
· ST. PATRICK"

PREFACE

THE opening sentence is copied from the preface to St. Luke's Gospel.

"*Like bringing boys into a council-meeting*," evidently an Irish proverbial saying. "Ut deducuntur pueri in ambiteathrum." *Amphitheatrum* probably represents the Irish *aonach*, assembly.

CHAPTER I

For Patrick's family and birthplace, see notes on Conf. 1.

A certain chieftain. The name Miliucc is not mentioned till Chapter XI.

The maxim of the Psalmist. Ps cxi. (cx) 10, "The fear of the Lord is the beginning of wisdom."

The angel Victoricus. See note on Conf. 23.

Sailed to Britain. This is a mistake, due to a misunderstanding of Conf. 23, "And again, after a few years, I was in Britain." Gaul was the destination of the traders. See notes on Conf 19

CHAPTER II

He had compassion on the multitude. Read *turbæ* for *turmæ*. There is an allusion to Matt. xv. 32.

Troubled in spirit. Cf. Ps. li. (l.) 17, "The sacrifice of God is a troubled spirit," *spiritus contribulatus.*

Patrick tasted nought of this food. According to his own account (Conf. 19), the wild honey was the only food he eschewed.

CHAPTER III

Muirchu has misunderstood Conf. 21. The "second captivity" there mentioned was his enforced stay with the sailors after they landed in Gaul.

CHAPTER IV

After a few years. Tirechán sums up the history of Patrick between his escape from Ireland and his return as missionary bishop thus: "For seven more years he journeyed on foot and by sea, on the waves,

in plains, and in mountain valleys, through Gaul and the whole of
Italy and in the islands which are in the Tyrrhene Sea, as he said
himself in his enumeration of his labours [viz. one of the *Dicta Patricii*].
Now he was for thirty years in one of those islands, which is called
Aralanensis [Lérins], as Bishop Ultan assured me" (fol. 9 r⁰ *b*).

CHAPTER V

Thirty years of age. Muirchu implies that Patrick had spent the
preceding seven years in Britain ; Tirechán, on the contrary, says that
they were spent in travel before he settled down at Lérins.

In Eph. iv. 13, which is quoted here, the word rendered *stature* in
E.V. is one that is rendered *age* elsewhere ; and so Muirchu understood
the Latin version, *ætatis*. By a fantastic exegesis, "the age of the
fulness of Christ" was connected with the fact that Jesus was thirty
years old when He began to teach (Luke iii. 23).

CHAPTER VI

The southern British sea is St. George's Channel, between England
and France.

Germanus, born probably about A D. 378, was a man of good family
who became one of the six "dukes," or governors, of Gaul. Amator,
Bishop of Autissiodorum (Auxerre), the chief town of his province,
forcibly ordained him in 418. In the same year Amator died after
providing that Germanus should be elected his successor. In 429,
Germanus, accompanied by Lupus, Bishop of Troyes, went to Britain
on a mission to stamp out the Pelagian heresy, which was distressing
the British Church. According to Constantius, who wrote a Life of
Germanus about A.D. 488, Germanus and Lupus were asked to come
by a synod of British bishops. This is Bede's account too (i. 17).
But Prosper of Aquitaine, a contemporary writer, says that Pope
Celestine "at the suggestion of the deacon Palladius, sent Germanus
as his representative into Britain" The mission was completely suc-
cessful. The enemies of the Church were crushed at a conference held
at St Albans, and the enemies of the State, the Picts and Saxons,
were routed in the Alleluia Victory, A D 430, organized by the two
bishops. In 447, Germanus visited Britain a second time and procured
the expulsion of the Pelagians He died in 448.

Muirchu has confused the relations of Patrick to Amator and to
Germanus. His statements are inconsistent. He gives an account of
Patrick's consecration as bishop by Amator, in Chapter IX, after a
parenthetical mention of his consecration by Germanus, in Chapter VIII.
It is very probable that Patrick did visit Auxerre during Amator's lifetime, and that Amator ordained him deacon and priest. "There is
evidence which points to the conclusion that Auxerre was a resort of
Irish Christians for theological study" (Bury, *St. Patrick*, p 49) ; and
we can without difficulty accept Muirchu's statement that Patrick studied
under Germanus. "He read the Canon with Germanus, this is what
writings narrate" (Hymn *Genair Patraic*). But the length of his
stay at Auxerre can hardly have been as much as fifteen years. If we

adopt 389, with Prof. Bury, as the year of Patrick's birth, 411 or 412 would be the year of his landing in Gaul; and we must allow for a long stay at Lérins.

CHAPTER VII

To go, and with the Gospel net, etc. This is an echo of the Hymn of St. Sechnall, iv.,

"Dominus illum elegit ut doceret barbaras
Nationes, ut piscaret per doctrinæ retia."

The boys and girls, etc. See note on Conf. 23, where Patrick plainly says that this vision took place in Britain, not in Gaul.

CHAPTER VIII

The journey which he had begun, viz. from Auxerre to Britain, not the journey to Rome, the interruption of which was noted in Chapter VI.

Germanus sent, etc. The sequence of events was probably as follows: When Palladius had been consecrated, Patrick and Segitius were sent by Germanus to Ireland to work under him, Patrick being probably designated eventually to succeed Palladius. Then when the intelligence of the death of Palladius reached Patrick, while on his way to some seaport of Gaul, he turned back to Auxerre, and was there consecrated by Germanus as bishop-in-Ireland.

They knew. Read *certi enim erant,* for *certe enim erat,* with Bury (*St. Patrick,* p. 345).

The first sea. A traveller from Ireland to Rome may cross two seas, viz that between Ireland and Britain, and that between Britain and the continent of Europe.

The country of the Britons. B reads, "of the Picts." Bury (*St Patrick,* p 55) thinks that the reading of B is in agreement with the actual facts. There was a colony of Picts in Dalaradia (South Antrim); and Bury supposes that there were Christians amongst them whom Palladius desired to visit. If this be so, Palladius was not abandoning his work when he died, but prosecuting it. Muirchu perhaps thought only of Picts as living in North Britain. But if a man were anxious to get to Rome from Ireland as quickly as possible, he would hardly go round by Scotland.

CHAPTER IX

Amathorex. Zimmer (*Nennius Vindicatus,* p. 123, note, quoted by Bury, *St. Patrick,* p. 347) has shewn that Muirchu's *Amathorege* represents the Irish form *Amatorig* for *Amator* (see note above, p 122).

Ebmoria has not been identified. Probus gives the name as *Euboria,* and B as *Curbia.* It must have lain between Auxerre and the English Channel. Bury suggests Ebroica, *i. e.* Evreux (*St. Patrick,* p. 347).

Auxilius. The Annals of Ulster, *s.a.* 439, state that Auxilius and Iserninus did not reach Ireland till seven years after Patrick. The name of Auxilius is preserved in that of a church founded by him near Naas,—Killishea, or Kill-ossy.

I

Iserninus was an Irishman whose "native name was Fith. He was born in the neighbourhood of Clonmore on the borders of Carlow and Wicklow" (Bury, *St. Patrick*, p. 164). He was consecrated by Patrick at Kilcullen, Co. Kildare.

Auxilius and Iserninus, whenever they joined Patrick in Ireland, seem to have been his most important coadjutors. Their names, and no others, are joined with his in the preamble to the Irish Canons (see Introduction, p. 28).

The presence of Iserninus, an Irish Christian, at Auxerre before A.D. 432, is one of the many indications of the existence of Christian communities in Ireland before Patrick.

Thou art a priest, etc. Ps. cx. (cix.) 4.

CHAPTER X

Prof. Bury has pointed out (*Guardian* for November 20, 1901) that this chapter was originally intended to follow Chapter XIV. The words *in the aforesaid country*, i. e. Ireland, are not appropriate in the present arrangement of the text.

Temoria = Tara. For a full and accurate account of this place, see papers by Dr. Petrie on the History and Antiquities of Tara Hill, *Transactions*, *R.I.A.* xviii., and by Prof. R. A. S. Macalister, in *Proceedings*, *R.I.A.*, xxxiv. C 10, 11: "Temair Breg; a Study of the Remains and Traditions of Tara."

Loiguire is the spelling in A. He was, for his age, an enlightened monarch. He came to terms with Patrick, and tolerated Christianity, though he did not embrace it himself (see note on Chap. XXI.) Under his auspices, the Code of the Laws of Ireland, known as the Senchus Mór, was drawn up. He reigned from 428 to 463.

Neill, or Niall, was High-king from 379 to 405. When Patrick came to Ireland, Loiguire's cousin, Amolngaid, was King of Connaught; another son of Niall, Conall, ruled in the territory still called Tyrconnell, and other sons were kings of lesser kingdoms in Meath (Bury, *St. Patrick*, p. 72).

Lothroch (*or Lochru*) *and Lucetmæl* (*or Ronal*). In Tirechán's narrative, there are "three magicians brothers, sons of one man. Their names and race are as follows: Cruth, Loch, Lethlanu, of the race of Runtir." Prof. Macalister (*op. cit.*, p. 333) holds that the names are not personal, but the names of three sacred stones at Tara. "Móel, Blocc, and Bluicne became the stock names for druids at Temair, so important were the stones associated with them." "Lochru et Lucetmael . . . are simply corruptions of [B]luicne et [B]locc et Mael."

Brought from a long distance, etc.—*for ever and ever*. The arrangement of these clauses in A suggests a rhythmical source.

Adze-head Asciciput (A) = asciæ caput (B nearly). This allusion to the strange appearance of the Christian monks is proof that the druidical tonsure, of the front of the head from ear to ear, was not the tonsure of St. Patrick. The early Christian tonsure was of the whole head. It is not certain at what date the coronal tonsure (first mentioned by Gregory of Tours) was introduced into the West. It is impossible not to believe that St. Patrick's tonsure was that of his friends in Gaul. Yet the Celtic tonsure, which was condemned by the Roman party in the seventh century, was the druidical tonsure. It is probable that the pre-Patrician Christian communities in Ireland conformed to druidical practice in this respect, and that the fashion introduced by Patrick did not prevail until reintroduced in the seventh century.

The term *Mael* describes a man tonsured in the druidical style. The name of Patrick's driver, Totmael (Totus Caluus), is significant, as descriptive of a man with no hair left on his head (see further, p. 133, and Bury, *St. Patrick*, pp. 239 ff.).

The original Irish of another version of this prophecy is preserved in a note on the Hymn, *Genair Patraicc*. Prof. Atkinson translates it as follows :—

> Adze-head will come
> Over mad-head sea,
> His cloak hole-head,
> His staff crook-head,
> His table in the west of his house ;
> All his household will answer, Amen, Amen.

There is nothing in Muirchu corresponding to line 2 of this, and line 5 is different. But line 3 gives the key to the interpretation of Muirchu's "*ex sua domu capite perforato.*" Prof. Atkinson misquotes this as *et sua*, etc. I would adopt *et* as a certain conjecture for *ex* ; and I take *domu*, house, to refer to the cloak or chasuble worn by the Christian priest, as is plainly expressed in the extant Irish form. *Casula*, chasuble, is in fact a diminutive from *casa*, a cottage. See *Irish Liber Hymnorum*, ii. 181 f.

There is some uncertainty as to the connexion of the words *ex anteriore parte domus suæ*. Dr. Gwynn takes *anteriore* here as *orientali*, comparing Chapter XI, where Inispatrick is called the *anterior insula* of the group, and this is also the rendering of *Vitæ* ii. iv. v. It is also to be noted that the extant Irish version of the prophecy emphasizes the *place* of the *mensa*, though it differs by calling it "the west of his house." Miss Hull informs me that in Irish the *back-part* or *behind* the house is always spoken of as the West (*Siar*), irrespective of its actual position. On the other hand, the meaning might be that the congregation were at the front part of the house, where one enters the church, the *mensa* being at the other end. Perhaps the words, "He will chant impiety" have dropped out, or have been deleted, from the Irish form ; and we should connect "in the west of his house" with "all his household."

CHAPTER XI

The Country of the Coolenni. Cuallan, in Co. Wicklow, Fercullen.

The Mouth of the Dee· Inbher Dee ; now the Vartry river, which runs into the sea at Wicklow.

According to Tirechán, the first spot of Irish soil that Patrick touched was the islands off Skerries, eighteen miles north of Dublin : "Patrick came with Gauls to the islands of Maccuchor, and [in particular] to the most easterly island which is called the Island of Patrick [Inis-Patrick]. . . . He landed at the plain of Breg [Eastern Meath]." Tirechán then proceeds at once with the Patrician foundations in Meath, and the story of Patrick's first Easter and his encounter with the magicians at Tara. Muirchu, on the other hand, states that Patrick merely touched at Inis-Patrick, and sailed north at once.

A twofold ransom "geminum servitutis premium." This seems an echo of S. Sechnall's Hymn, xxi., "Qui de gemino captivos liberat servitio."

Breg (Magh-Breagh) is the eastern part of north Co. Dublin, Meath, and part of Louth.

The Conaille country. "Conalneos fines," is part of Co. Louth.

The Ulaid country "fines Ulathorum," here means Co. Down. Originally, Ulaid, or Ulidia, embraced the whole province now called Ulster.

A lough which is Brene: "fretum Brene," Strangford Lough.

Slain. The river Slaney, now commonly called the Scadden.

Patrick's Barn "Orreum Patricii," Sabhall Phadraig, now Saul.

The Cruidneni. The Cruithnii, or Cruthenii, were a tribe of Picts who had settled in Dalaradia, *i e.* South Antrim and Down.

Mount Mis "Mons Miss," now Slemish, which is a contraction of Sliabh (= mountain) and Mis. This hill (the summit of which is 1,437 feet high), "like an inverted bowl, round and wide-brimmed" (Bury), is three miles distant from "a second mountain," Scirte, now Skerry. The river Braid runs between them. Skerry was also a haunt of Patrick's when a slave. "Then the angel of the Lord visited him in dreams on the summit of Mount Scirte, beside Mount Mis" (Tirechán). This story of the angel ascending into heaven from Skerry is repeated in Book ii. 15, where Muirchu gives the name of the second mountain as *Scirit.*

CHAPTER XII

A spot which is now marked by a cross. This is commemorated in the name of the parish of Cross. It is on the south-western side of the hill.

The Plain of Inis "campum Inis"; in Irish, Magh-Inis, the island plain, the district south of Strangford Lough, now the barony of Lecale in the Co. Down.

CHAPTER XIV

Leaving on the right hand, etc. This sentence, awkwardly expressed and condensed in the original, seems to mean (1) that Patrick was now sailing in a southerly direction, so that the territory of Cos. Down and Louth were now on his right, whereas they had been on his left, when sailing north. (2) There is also a play on the ethical sense of *dexter* and *lævus,* of good and bad omen respectively. (3) He was not abandoning Louth and Down, but postponing the evangelization of that country to a time when he would be able to "fulfil his ministry" (2 Tim iv. 5).

Colpdi, the River Boyne.

The Graves of the Men of Fecc, near Slane, are mentioned again in Chapter XVI.

The prophet. Ps. l. (xlix.) 14, "Offer unto God the sacrifice of praise, and pay thy vows unto the Most High."

CHAPTER XV

According to Prof. Bury (*St. Patrick*, pp. 107, 303), Muirchu (or his source), by a clever literary device, unites the features of two heathen festivals, on neither of which Easter could fall. It was at Beltane, the first day of summer (May 1st), that the fire was lighted at Tara, and it was at Samhain, the first day of winter (November 1st), when the High-Kings held festival at Tara. Prof. Macalister, however (*op. cit.* pp. 367 ff.), defends the accuracy of Muirchu. He suggests that there was most probably a great feast at Tara at the vernal equinox, the re-birth of the sun-god, corresponding to the festival of his death, on 1st November. "Easter in A.D. 433, the year of St. Patrick's coming to Temair, fell upon 26 March. As the Paschal Fire was lit on Easter Eve, the festival which the saint violated was held on 25 March. This is the very date on which, in many places, the resurrection of the deity of vegetation was celebrated."

St. Patrick kindled a divine fire. Tirechán (fol. 10 vᵒ *a*), speaking of Bishop Kannanus, who is buried at Duleek, and who was ordained on this occasion by Patrick, says, "It was he who carried with him the first blessed fire, and carried home from the hands of Patrick the first wax candles to kindle a blessed smoke under the eyes and nostrils of the heathen folk and of King Loiguire and his magicians."

CHAPTER XVI

Nine chariots. B and *Vita* ii. read "nine times three," *curribus ternis novies.*

Turning to the left, or contrariwise to the sun's course, in order to win magic power over them who had kindled the fire (Bury, *St. Patrick*, p. 105). Prof. Macalister suggests that this performance took place in the stone circle at Tara called the Deisel (*op. cit.* p. 368).

CHAPTER XVII

Some put their trust, etc. Ps. xx. (xix.) 7. Patrick substitutes *ambulabimus* for *invocabimus;* "we will walk in the name," for "we will call upon the name."

Ercc the son of Daig. The incident of Ercc rising up in token of respect is placed by Tirechán (fol 10 vᵒ *a*) in connexion with a second visit of Patrick to Tara: "And he entered the royal palace; and none rose up before him save one only, that is Hercus, a man busy about sacred things. And he said to him, Why didst thou alone rise up in honour of my God in me? And Hercus said to him, I know not what, I see sparks of fire mounting from thy lips to my lips. Moreover the Saint said, Wilt thou accept the baptism of the Lord which is with me? He replied, I will accept it. And they came to the fountain called in Irish Loíg-Les, but by us, the Calf of the Cities [vitulus civitatum]. And when he had opened the book and was baptizing the man Hercus, he heard men behind his back laughing amongst themselves as they beheld this thing; for they knew, not what he was doing." Then follows the account of the conversation in which Patrick heard the Wood of Fochlath mentioned.

Lochru was insolent. In Tírechán (fol. 10 r⁰ *a*) this incident follows immediately after the burning of the other magician, which Muirchu relates in Chapter XX: "And Patrick raised his hands to God around the magician Loch Letheus, and said, O my Lord, cast away from me this dog which barks against thy face and me; let him depart in death. And all watched the magician as he was raised through the darkness of night almost to the heavens. But on its return, his corpse, stiffened with hail and snow and enveloped with sparks of fire, fell to the earth before the faces of them all. And his stone [*i. e.* the stone which marks the spot where he fell] is at the southern and eastern borders [of Tara] even to the present day; and I have seen it with mine own eyes."

CHAPTER XVIII

Let God arise, etc. Ps. lxviii. (lxvii.) 1.

And he bound . . . violence. This is the Old Latin rendering of the LXX of Exod. xiv. 25, where the E.V. is, "And he took off their chariot wheels, that they drave them heavily." The Vulgate is altogether different. Sabatier gives no more of the O.L. of the verse than " Et colligavit axes curruum eorum," from Hilary *in Ps* 118

The Mountain of Monduirn. Hogan suggests that this may represent either the country between Dublin and Drogheda, inhabited by the Mugdorni-Breg, or it may be a hill, Modhuirn, in the barony of Cremorne, Co. Monaghan.

Eight stags. The ancient Irish incantation, commonly called the *Lorica,* or Breastplate of St. Patrick, is also known as the *Faeth Fiada.* These words are generally rendered "the Deer's Cry," and connected with this story of Patrick's transformation of himself and his companions into deer (*Vit. Trip.,* i. 48). But see Introduction to the *Lorica,* p. 64.

CHAPTER XIX

Dubthach-maccu-Lugir, a poet; he was one of the compilers of the Senchus Mór, or Code of Laws, published in Loíguire's reign.

Fiace. First bishop of Sletty. An ancient Irish hymn concerning St. Patrick, called from its first words, *Genair Patraicc,* used to be ascribed to him. But the approximate date of the hymn, according to recent critics, is A.D. 800 (see Introduction, p. 25).

CHAPTER XX

Throw them into fire. Tírechán (fol. 10 r⁰ *a*) makes no mention of the wooden house in connexion with this ordeal: "Now the cloak of the magician was put on Benignus, and set on fire; and it was burnt to ashes.   But the holy child was, through his firm faith in God, kept whole in the sight of the King and of his people and of the magicians.   But when the cloak of Benignus, Patrick's son, was put around the magician, the magician was set on fire in the midst of them, and burnt up.   And Patrick said, In this hour is all the heathenism of Ireland burnt up."

Ye shall be judged, etc. For the reading here, see Bury, *Hermathena,* xxviii. p. 193.

Benineus is Benignus, who succeeded Patrick in the see of Armagh, A.D. 457.   Patrick resigned in his favour.   He was one of the compilers of the Senchus Mór.   He died in A D. 467   Tirechán (fol. 9 v° *a*) gives the following account of how Benignus joined Patrick's company.   Almost immediately after Patrick's first landing on the Meath coast, "at evening time he came to the mouth of the Ailbine [Delvin] to the house of a certain good man ; and he baptized him. And he found with him a son to whom he took a fancy.   And he gave him the name of Benignus, because he used to fondle with his hands the feet and breast of Patrick ; and would not sleep with his father and mother, but wept if he might not sleep with Patrick   Now when they arose in the morning, Patrick mounted his car when he had made an end of blessing the father of Benignus.   And he had one foot on the car and the other on the ground.   And the boy Benignus held Patrick's foot tightly with both hands, and cried, Let me go with Patrick my own father.   And Patrick said, Baptize him, and put him up into the car; for he is the heir of my kingdom.   This is Bishop Benignus, Patrick's successor in the church of Machæ "

Muirchu, in Chapter XXVIII, relates another incident about Benignus which commended him to Patrick as his successor.

"*And his heart was moved.*"   A quotation from Isaiah vii. 2

CHAPTER XXI

The account given by Tirechán (fol. 10 r° *b*) of Loiguire's attitude towards Christianity is both more credible than that of Muirchu, and more creditable to the King : " He journeyed a second time to the city of Temro [Tara], to Loiguire son of Neill, because he had made a covenant with him that he should not be killed in his kingdom.   But he was unable to believe [*i. e.* confess Christ], saying, For Neill, my father, did not permit me to believe ; but [ordered] that I be buried on the summit of Temro, as men standing ready for battle.   (For it is the custom of the heathen to be buried armed, with weapons ready for use, confronting each other until the day of *erdathe,* as the magicians express it, that is, the day of the Lord's judgement.)   I am the son of Neill ; and [so] the son of Dunlinge [is buried] on Maistin in the plain of the Liphi, because of [our] implacable hatred."

Dunlinge was the King of Leinster, whose seat was at Maistin, now Mullaghmast, in Co. Kildare, in the valley of the Liffey.   The Kings of Meath were buried armed, in standing posture, facing south, and the Kings of Leinster were buried similarly, facing north, each faithful in death to the hereditary feud between their houses.

CHAPTER XXII

The closing words of this chapter are taken from the end of St. Mark's Gospel. Here Book I of Muirchu's *Life* ends, according to the arrangement of B (see above, p. 69).

CHAPTER XXIII

Maccu Greccæ means *Son of Prey*. In the Irish *Vita Tripartita* (i. 221), he is called *Son of Death*. Prof. Bury (*St. Patrick*, p. 267) suggests that this Maccuil may be the same as a figure in Irish mythology, of the same name, adapted to the Patrician story. It is perhaps indicative of an Irish metrical source that, in A, the passage *He was depraved . . . conscience*, is set out in two columns, noun under noun, and adjective under adjective.

In Druim-maccu-Echaid. So Dr. Gwynn. A has Hindruim moccuechach, which Hogan, following Reeves, identifies with Nendrum, or Mahee Island, *i.e.* the island of St. Mochay, in Strangford Lough (Reeves, *Eccl. Antiq. of Down*, p. 187, ff.). But Muirchu's description of the place is drawn from his own imagination.

The vilest signs of cruelty. In A, over the words *signa sumens*, is the Irish gloss, *diberca*, which Dr. Gwynn renders "robbers' badges."

Bear a mark of thy sin on thy head. This is probably an instance of a primitive custom, in accordance with which manslayers bore a mark painted on their foreheads to avert the wrath of the ghost of the slain man, or to ward off ill-luck of other kinds. See Frazer on the Mark of Cain, in *Folk-lore of the Old Testament*, i. p. 78 ff.

Evonia, the Isle of Man.

A man dressed in only one garment: "virum unius habitus." B reads *hujus* for *unius*, "dressed in this fashion."

Bishop of Man For the word *dimane* (A), which Dr. Gwynn renders "of Man," Hogan suggests three explanations: (i) perfectus, (ii) Dei monachus, (iii) valde felix.

Arddæ Huimnonn = the Height of Evonia. So Gwynn; Hogan explains it as "the Height of Mona."

CHAPTER XXIV

This chapter embodies the Armagh tradition concerning the foundation of the See by St. Patrick, the date of which, according to the Annals of Ulster, is A.D. 444 (see Todd, *St. Patrick*, p. 469 ff). Daire was a much more important personage than Muirchu's language about him would suggest. "It seems that he was in any case chief of the Hy-Nialláin [O'Neill-land], and probable that he was also King of Oriel." It is said that he "co-operated with Loigaire and Corc [of Munster] in initiating the Senchus Mór" (see Bury, *St. Patrick*, p. 308).

In the country of Airthir: "in regione Orientalium." This is the district known as Airthir, the baronies of Upper and Lower Orior in Co. Armagh, the eastern portion of the kingdom of Oriel, or South Ulster.

The Ridge of the Willow: "Dorsum salicis," Druim sailech, Drumsallagh.

The Graves of the Relics: "Fertæ martyrum." The rendering, *Church of the Relics*, is that of Dr. Gwynn. Reeves (*Adamnan*, p. 314, note *m.*) gives examples of the use of *martyria* in the sense of *ossa.*

Ardd Machœ, The Height of Macha, who is said to have reigned there as queen.

Like a deaf man, etc. Ps. xxxviii. (xxxvii.) 13.

Three gallons, "metritas ternas." A *metretes* is really equivalent to nine gallons; but the pot which Daire offered Patrick could hardly have held twenty-seven gallons.

Grazacham represents a hurried pronunciation of *gratias agam. Deo gratias* and *gratias ago* occur constantly in St. Patrick's Latin writings (see note on Conf. 19).

In so far as I possess it · "Quantum habeo." A man could not dispose of his land without the consent of the other members of the tribe.

Like a gentle and tame sheep. Read with Prof Bury (from Probus), "velut [mitissim]a man[sue]tissimaque ovis" (*Hermathena*, xxviii. p. 185).

CHAPTER XXV

The Hill of the Ox: "Collum bovis." This place is mentioned again in Book II, Chapter XIII, where it seems to be a portion of Strangford Lough. This seems fatal to the suggestion that it is Drumbo, which is inland. Reeves thought it was the Bay of Dundrum.

Mudebroth. The meaning of this expletive, which occurs in Chapter XXVI, in the form *Mudebrod*, is uncertain. The scholiast on the Hymn *Genair Patraicc* rendered it, "By my God of judgment"; Stokes, "My God's doom"; but Prof. Atkinson says, "The oath *Dar mo De broth* is mere jargon. *De broth* ought to mean something like 'God's doom-day'; but even then there would be a difficulty, because the genitive Dé could not precede its governing noun" (*Liber Hymn.* ii. 178, 179).

CHAPTER XXVI

A fruitful land, etc. Ps. cvii. (cvi.), 34.

CHAPTER XXVII

Moneisen. The name is spelt *Monesan* in B. This chapter is the first in Book II., according to the arrangement of the Life in B. This accounts for the opening words, which cannot have been in the archetype of A 1.

The example of the patriarch Abraham, who, according to Jewish tradition, was persecuted for abandoning the idolatrous worship of his ancestors to embrace a pure monotheism (cf. Josh. xxiv 2).

Muirchu's story of Moneisen has some features in common with that of Ethne and Fedelm, told by Tirechán (fol. 12 ro a). There is the same curiosity respecting topics of Natural Religion on the part of the heathen maiden, and there is death following, immediately as it seems, after baptism.   These points do not appear in St. Patrick's reference to the *benedicta Scotta* of Conf. 42.

Tirechán's story is as follows:

"Then St. Patrick came before the rising of the sun to a fountain which is called Clebach, on the side of Crochan [Rathcrochan] looking towards the sunrising.   And they sat beside the fountain.

"And, lo, two daughters of King Loiguire, Ethne the fair and Fedelm the golden-haired, came to the fountain to wash in the morning, as is the wont of women.   And they found beside the fountain the holy synod of bishops with Patrick.   And they were at a loss to know where they were, or in what shape they were, or of what people they were, or to what country they belonged.   But they judged them to be fairy men, or to be of the earth gods, or to be an apparition

"And the girls said to them, Where are ye? and whence come ye? And Patrick said to them, It were better for you to confess the true God, our God, than to ask questions about our race.

"The elder [prima] girl said, Who is God?   And where is God? And whose is God [*or*, of what nature is God]?   And where is His dwelling?   Has your God sons and daughters, gold and silver?   Does He live for ever?   Is He beautiful?   Had His Son many foster-fathers? Are His daughters dear and beautiful to the men of this world?   Is He in heaven or in earth?   in the sea?   in the rivers?   in the mountains?   in the valleys?   Tell us the knowledge of Him.   How shall He be seen? How is He loved?   How is He found?   Is it in youth, is it in old age, that He is found?

"Then St. Patrick, full of the Holy Spirit, answered and said, As for our God, He is the God of all men.   He is God of heaven and earth, of sea and rivers; He is the God of sun and moon; of all the stars.   He is the God of the lofty mountains and of the lowly valleys.   God, above the heaven and in the heaven and under the heaven, has His dwelling around heaven and earth and sea and all that in them is.   He inspires all things; He quickens all things; He transcends all things; He sustains all things.   He gives its light to the sun; He veils the light and knowledge of the night.[1]   He made fountains in the parched land, and dry islands in the midst of the sea; and He appointed the stars to serve the greater lights.

"He hath a Son, co-eternal with Himself and co-equal with Himself [consimilem].   The Son is not younger than the Father, nor the Father older than the Son; and the Holy Spirit breathes in them; nor are Father, Son, and Holy Spirit divided.

"Now I wish to unite you to the heavenly King, inasmuch as ye are daughters of an earthly king.   Believe.

---

[1] Lumen noctis et notitias valat.   Read *velat*, with Hogan.   It means that the obscurity of night, which hinders cognition by the senses, is God's doing.   Cf. Is. xiv. 7: "I form the light, and create darkness."

"And the girls said, as with one mouth and heart, That we may be able to believe on the heavenly King, do thou teach us with the utmost care. That we may see Him face to face, do thou direct us; and we shall do whatsoever thou sayest.

"And Patrick said, Do ye believe that by baptism ye cast away the sin of your father and mother? They answered, We believe.

"Do ye believe in repentance after sin? We believe.

"Do ye believe in life after death? Do ye believe in a resurrection at the Day of Judgment? We believe.

"Do ye believe in the unity of the Church? We believe.

So they were baptized; and a white veil was put over their heads. And they demanded to see the face of Christ. And the Saint said to them, Unless ye taste of death, ye cannot see the face of Christ, nor unless ye receive the Sacrifice. And they answered, Give us the Sacrifice, that we may see the Son, our spouse. And they received the Eucharist of God, and they slept in death. And they placed them in one bed, covered with garments. And their friends made a wailing and great lamentation.

"And the magician Caplit came, who was foster-father to one of the maidens; and he wept. And Patrick preached to him, and he believed, and the hairs of his head were removed. And his brother Mael came; and he said, My brother believed in Patrick; but so shall not I; but I shall bring him back to heathenism. And he spake roughly to Mathous [i. e. Benignus (?)] and to Patrick. And Patrick spoke to him, and preached to him, and converted him to the repentance that comes from God. And the hairs of his head were removed; that is to say, the magician's fashion, which had been before seen on his head, which is called airbacc giunnæ [tonsure of the hair in front]. Hence the saying which is better known than any other in the Irish language, 'Mael is like Caplit' [Similis est Caluus contra Caplit], because they believed in God.

"And the days of wailing for the King's daughters were ended; and they buried them beside the fountain of Clebach; and they made a circular ditch like a ferta; for so did the Irish and the heathen folk make them.

"Now it is called by us Relic, that is, the Remains of the Maidens. And [the ferta] was dedicated to God and to Patrick (with the bones of the holy maidens), and to his heirs after him for ever. And he made a [church] of earth on that spot."

Dr. Gwynn (op. cit., p. 454) says that the proverb Mael is like Caplit, applies to two who, after opposition, come to agree. Prof. Bury sees in it an allusion to the rival methods of tonsure, Druidic and Christian. Mael refers to the tonsure of the front of the head from ear to ear; while Caplit—which he derives from capillatus, in the sense of de-capillatus—refers to the tonsure prevalent at that time in the Christian Church, of the whole head. It is probable that in the pre-Patrician Christian communities in Ireland the native Druidical tonsure was adopted by the monks. Perhaps the proverb originated in a cynical reflection that monks of all creeds are practically indistinguishable: "New Presbyter is but old Priest writ large."

CHAPTER XXIX

Coroticus. Coirthech is the spelling in the title, derived from A 1. B has *Corictic* in the chapter itself (see notes on the Letter, p 119).

BOOK II

The note printed here at the end of Book I, and which in A follows the Table of Book I, suggests that the matter contained in Book II was *not* derived from Ædh. It was drawn probably from a Ulidian source. This is almost certainly the case as regards Chapters IV—XIV, the account of Patrick's death and burial. In the margin of A the numerals VI and VIII are found opposite the first words of Chapters IX and XI respectively. This is a trace of an old source-document in which our present Chapter IV was I.

CHAPTER I

He used to sing, etc., is a quotation from stanza xxii. of the Hymn of St. Sechnall · "Ymnos cum Apocalipsi psalmosque cantat Dei."

CHAPTER II

Tirechán (fol. 14 r° *b*) has another version of this story : "And he came to Magh Finn [Albus Campus] in the regions of the Hy-Many [South Roscommon], and he found there a sign of the cross of Christ, [*i. e.* a cross erected] and two new sepulchres. And from his car the Saint said, Who is buried here? And a voice answered from the sepulchre, Lo, I am a heathen man. And the Saint responded, Why is the holy cross fixed beside thee? And he answered again, Because the mother of the man who is buried by my side made request that the sign of the cross might be placed by the sepulchre of her son ; and a silly and stupid man placed it beside me. And St. Patrick leaped from his car, and seized the cross, and pulled it out of the heathen grave-mound, and placed it over the face of the baptized man, and mounted his car, and prayed to God silently. When he had said, *Deliver us from evil,* his driver said to him, What ! why didst thou address a heathen unbaptized man?

"Because I sigh over a man who is without baptism.

"It were better in God's sight to give him a blessing in lieu of baptism, and to pour baptismal water over the sepulchre of the dead man.

"And he made him no answer. I imagine that the reason why he left him was because God willed not to save him."

Immediately before this, Tirechán has a story of a long-dead heathen whom Patrick raised, and baptized with a view to his greater ease, and then re-buried.

The driver, "auriga," of St. Patrick's car was named Totmael (*Totus* and *mael* = caluus). This curiously hybrid compound name is, in A, written over the words *Totus Caluus* in the following extract from Tirechán (fol. 13 v° a) :—

" And Patrick journeyed to Mount Egli [Croagh-Patrick], to fast on it forty days and forty nights, observing the discipline of Moses and of Elijah and of Christ.   And his driver died in Muiriscc Aigli [Murrisk], that is, the plain between the sea and Aigleus [Croagh-Patrick].   And he buried Totus Caluus the driver ; and he heaped stones around his tomb ; and he said, May it so remain for ever ! and it shall be visited by me in the last days " (see Bury, *St. Patrick*, p. 242).

CHAPTER III

Gideon's bowl and fleece.   Muirchu's recollection of the story is confused.   In the second sign granted to Gideon, "it was dry upon the fleece " ; but in the first sign, he "wringed the dew out of the fleece, a bowl full of water " (Judges vi. 38).

Helper . . . in times of trouble (Ps. ix. 10).

CHAPTER VI

Thy jurisdiction : " ordinatio tua," the primacy which is the privilege of Patrick's successors in the see of Armagh.   •

The hymn is that composed by St. Sechnall or Secundinus.

And ye shall sit and judge, etc. (Matt. xix. 28 ; Luke xxii. 30).   The germ of the idea here expressed is found in the last line of St. Sechnall's Hymn, "Cum apostolis regnabit sanctus super Israel," which is explained in the gloss thus : " Regnabit Patricius in die judicii."   Lines 51, 52 of the Hymn *Genair Patraicc* combine the first two petitions : " A hymn which thou hast chosen in thy lifetime shall be a lorica of protection for all ; Around thee in the Day of Judgment men of Ireland will go to doom."

Another set of Petitions of Patrick, three in number, is found in the Book of Armagh, fol. 15 v° b, and in the *Historia Brittonum* (see Bury, *St. Patrick*, p. 277) : "These are the three Petitions of Patrick, as they have been handed down to us Irish folk :—

" Making request 1.   That each one of us, on doing penance, even at the end of his life, should be accepted at the Day of Judgment, so as not to be shut up in hell.   This is the first.

" 2. The second.   That barbarous peoples should not rule over us for ever.

" 3. That none of us, that is, of the Irish, should be alive seven years before the Day of Judgment ; because seven years before the Judgment they will be destroyed by the sea.   This is the third."

CHAPTER VIII

Night did not come down.   Muirchu here exhibits his knowledge of the classics, combining a quotation from Virgil with one from Sedulius, a Christian poet of the fifth century.

1. *Æn.* viii. 369 : Nox ruit, et fuscis tellurem amplectitur alis.

2. Sedulius, *Carmen Paschale*, iii. 219 :

" Iamque senescentem gelidi sub cærula ponti
Oceano rapiente diem, cum pallor adesset
Noctis et astriferas induceret Hesperus umbras,
Discipuli, solo terris residente magistro
Undosum petiere salum," etc.

For these references I am indebted to Dr. L. C. Purser.

Now if any one. This paragraph was misplaced in A, in which it is written in the Table of Contents between titles 14 and 15 (see Gwynn, *op. cit.*, p. xxxvii. note 1).

CHAPTER IX

The title of this chapter is supplied by Dr. Gwynn (*op. cit.* p. xxxix).

Tassach, Bishop of Raholp or Rathcolpa. He had been originally Patrick's "artificer, who made altars and other things which were needed for his religious rites" (Bury, *St. Patrick*, p. 90).

CHAPTER X

See the smell, etc. (Gen. xxvii. 27).

CHAPTER XI

Let two unbroken oxen, etc. This was on the analogy of the Philistines' disposition of the ark of Jehovah (1 Sam. vi. 7).

Clocher . . . Findubair. Neither of these places has been identified.

Dun-Lethglaisse is Downpatrick.

Where Patrick was buried. A note in the Book of Armagh (fol. 15 v° b), and in the *Historia Brittonum*, says : "In four points Patrick was like unto Moses :—(1) First, he heard an angel [speaking to him] out of a bush ; (2) he fasted forty days and forty nights ; (3) because he passed 120 years in the present life; (4) where his bones are no man knoweth."

It is plain that he died at Saul. That is implied in Chapter V. He had been living there since his retirement, for some three or four years ; and it would be natural to suppose that he was buried where he had spent his last years. This is plainly stated in a note in A, which immediately follows that just quoted : " Colomb-cille, under the inspiration of the Holy Spirit, showed the place of Patrick's burial ; he confirms [the tradition as to] where it is; that is, in Sabhul Patrick, that is, in the church nearest the sea, where there is a gathering together of relics, that is, of the bones of Colomb-cille from Britain, and a gathering together of all the saints of Ireland in the Day of Judgment."

This note is not part of the work of Tirechán ; but was probably due to the scribe of A, Ferdomnach. It is at least evidence that in his time the Ulidian tradition as to the Saint's burial-place was uncertain. The miraculous details associated with the claims of Downpatrick naturally prejudice the modern mind in favour of Saul. And the secular insignificance of Saul constitutes an argument in the same direction. Downpatrick was a royal seat ; and if Patrick had really been buried there, it is not easy to see how the Saul tradition could have arisen.

CHAPTER XIII

The Ui-Neill lived in the counties of Tyrone, Donegal, and Londonderry.

The Hill of the Ox : "Collum Bovis" (see note on Book I, Chapter XXV).

CHAPTER XIV

The River Cabcenne. This has not been identified.

CHAPTER XV

The title of this chapter as given here is taken from B, in which it follows Chapter XII of Book I. The title in A is *De diligentia orationis*, almost identical with that of Chapter I.

INDEX

ADAMNAN's synod at Birr, 71
Ædh, Bishop of Sletty, 68 f, 71, 101, 134
Aigleus *or* Aigli, Mount. See Croagh-Patrick
Ail, 100. See Alcluith
Ailbine, river (Delvin), 129
Airthir (Orior), 95, 107, 108, 130
Alcluith (Dumbarton), 52 f, 111 f, 119
Alsiodorum, 76. See Auxerre
Amator *or* Amatborex, Bishop of Auxerre, 13 f, 78, 122, 123
Amolngid, King of Connaught, 10, 124
Arddæ-Huimnonn (Man), 94, 130
Ardd-Machæ. See Armagh
Armagh, see of, 20, 95, 96, 97, 105, 129, 130
—— Northern Church at, 97
—— Patrick desires to die there, 104
Armagh, Book of, 27
Augustine of Hippo, 12
Augustinus, disciple of Palladius, 78
Auxerre, 76, 122, 124
Auxilius, 28, 78, 123 f

Banavem Taberniæ, 31, 73, 111 f
Bede, 122
Beltane, 127
Benedictus, disciple of Palladius, 78
Benignus *or* Benineus, 64, 90, 100, 119, 128 f, 133
Biblical text used by Patrick, 1 ff
Birr, synod at, 71
Bordeaux, 114
Boyne, river, 113, 126
Braid, river, 126
Breg, 80, 83, 126
Brene (Strangford Lough), 80, 126
Brigid of Kildare, *Life* of, 70

Britain, revisited by Patrick, 38, 74, 121, 122
—— visited by Germanus, 122
Britanniæ, 4, 111, 115
Burial customs, 129, 133, 135
Bury, J. B., *Life of St. Patrick*, 27 f

Cabcenne, river, 108, 137
Calpurnius, father of Patrick, 31, 73, 110
Canons, Irish, 28, 124
Caplit, magician, 133. See Mael
Caredig, 52, 112
Celestine, Pope: connexion with Germanus' visit to Britain, 122; sends Palladius to Ireland, 77; connexion with Patrick, 16 f
Celibacy of the clergy, 4 f, 110 f
Celtic ecclesiastical usages, 18
Cinnu *or* Cymna, 117
Clebach, fountain, 132, 133
Clocher, 107, 136
Clonmore, 124
Cogitosus, father of Muirchu, 70, 72
Colgan, J., *Trias Thaumaturga*, 26
Collum Bovis, 97, 108, 131
Colpdi, river (Boyne), 83, 126
Columba (Colombcille), 136
Conail's oxen draw Patrick's bier, 107
Conaille country, 80, 126
Conall, of Tyrconnell, 124
Concessa, mother of Patrick, 73, 111
Confession of St. Patrick, 29 ff
Confirmation, 117
Conindri, bishop in Man, 94
Connaught, Patrick's work in, 9, 25
Constantius' *Life of Germanus*, 122

Coolenni, 80, 125
Coroticus, 4, 111 f, 119
—— Patrick's *Letter* to him, 52 ff, 100, 134
Cothraige, name of Patrick, 110
Creed, baptismal, 133
Croagh-Patrick, mountain, 8ff, 135
Crochan, 132
Crochan-Aigli, 8. See Croagh-Patrick
Cross, Patrick's veneration for, 102 f, 134
Cross, townland of, 81, 126
Cruidneni, 81, 126
Cruth, magician, 124
Cuallan, 125

Daire of Armagh, 95 ff, 130
Dalaradia, 123, 126
Daventry, 111
Decurions, 119
Dee, river (Vartry), 80, 125
Deer's Cry, 64, 128
Delvin, river, 129
Diberca, 130
Dichu, Patrick's first convert, 80 ff, 83, 105
Dicta Patricii, 11, 15 f, 67, 120
Dimane, 130
Dogs, Irish, 114
Dorsum Salicis, 95, 131
Downpatrick, 107, 136 f
Druim-maccu-Echaid, 92, 130
Drumbo, 131
Drumsallagh, 131
Dubthach-maccu-Lugir, poet, 25, 88, 128
Duleek, 127
Dumbarton. See Alcluith
Dundrum Bay, 131
Dun-Lethglaisse (Downpatrick), 107, 136
Dunlinge, King of Leinster, 129
Dunshaughlin, 22

Easter in A.D. 433, 127
Easter Fires, 127
Ebmoria, 78, 123
Egli, Mount, 8, 135. See Croagh-Patrick

Endeus, son of Amolngid, 10, 118
Ercc, son of Daig, 87, 127
Ethne and Fedelm, daughters of Loiguire, 62, 117, 132 f
Evonia (Ise of Man), 94, 130

Faeth Fiada, 64, 128
Fecc (Graves of the Men of Fecc), 83, 85, 127
Fedelm. See Ethne
Fercullen, 125
Ferdomnach the Scribe, 17, 20, 27, 136
Ferta (grave), 83, 85, 95, 127, 131, 133
Fiacc, Bishop of Sletty, 25, 88, 128
Fiacc, Hymn of. See *Genair Patraicc*
Findubair, 107, 136
Fith. See Iserninus
Fochlath *or* Foclut, Wood of, 6 f, 38 f, 77, 115, 118
Franks, 4, 58, 120

Gaul, 45, 58, 117, 119
Genair Patraicc, Hymn, 25 f, 128
—— quotations from it, 110 (*bis*), 111, 122, 135
Germanus, 11 ff, 76, 77, 122, 123
Grazacham, 96, 114, 131
Gwynn, Rev. John, edition of the *Book of Armagh*, 27

Habeo, use of in Low Latin, 113
Helias, 38, 75, 114
Hercaith, 17
Hercus (Ercc), 127
Hill of the Ox, 97, 108, 131
Historia Brittonum, 135, 136
Hogan, Rev. Edmund, edition of the Patrician Documents, 27
Hy-Many, 134
Hy-Niallain, 130. See Ui-Neill.
Hymus. See *Genair Patraicc* and Sechnall

Inis Patrick, island, 80, 126
Inis, Plain of (Magh-Inis), 82, 83, 94, 97, 126
Ireland, Patrick's names for, 112

Irenæus, 12, 112, 113
Iserninus, 28, 78, 124
Italy, 11

Jerome's revisions and translations
  of the Bible, 2
Jocelin (*Vita* vi.), 26, 110

Kannanus, 127
Kilcullen, 124
Killossy *or* Killishea, 123

Lecale, 126
Leo I, Pope: alleged visit of
  Patrick to, 17
Lérins, 11, 14, 114, 123
Lethanu, magician, 124
Liber Hymnorum, 24, 61
Liphi, river (Liffey), 129
Loch, magician, 124, 128 -
Lochru *or* Lothroch, magician,
  79, 85, 86, 124, 128
Loig-les, fountain, 128
Loiguire, High King, 78 f, 84–91,
  124, 129
Lorica, 61, 128
Lothroch.   See Lochru
Lucetmael *or* Ronal, magician,
  79, 85, 89 f, 124
Lupait, sister of Patrick, 111
Lupus, Bishop of Troyes, 122

Maccu-Chor, islands of, 125
Maccuil, 92 ff, 130
Machi, 104.   See Armagh
Mael, 124, 125, 133
" Mael is like Caplit," 133
Magh Finn, 134
Magh Inis.   See Inis, Plain of
Magonus, name of Patrick, 110
Mahee Island, 130
Maistin, 129
Man, Isle of, 94, 130
Marianus Scotus, 110, 111
Martin of Tours, 111
Martyria, 131
Mathous, 133
Metretes, 131
Michi, 104.   See Armagh
Miliucc, 80 ff, 113
Mis *or* Miss, Mount (Slemish),
  7 ff, 81, 109, 126

Mithraism, 4, 114, 118
Mochay St., Island of, 130
Monduirn, 87, 128
Moneisen *or* Monesan, 98 f, 117,
  131
Mudebrod or *Mudebroth*, 97, 98,
  131
Muirchu-maccu-Machtheni, 68 ff,
  101
Mullaghmast, 129
Murrisk, 135

Neill *or* Niall, 78, 124, 129
Nemthur, 111
Nendrum, 130
Nentria, 111
Ninian of Whithern, 5, 119

Odissus, 111
Oriel, 130
Orior, 130

Palladius, his interest in Britain,
  122; sent to Ireland, 16, 77;
  his death, 77 f, 123
Patrick: date of birth, 1; birth-
  place, 31, 73, 111 f; names,
  110; family, 31, 73, 110 f;
  early education, 112; self-de-
  preciation, 110, 112; place of
  captivity in Ireland, 6 ff, 115;
  escape to Gaul, 114; second (?)
  captivity, 38, 75, 114, 121;
  stay at Lérins, 11, 114, 122;
  stay at Auxerre, 76, 122; range
  of his studies, 11 f; revisits
  Britain, 13, 38, 75; missionary
  projects, 12 f, 115; ordination,
  13 f, 77 f, 123; connexion with
  Rome, 14 ff; lands in Ireland,
  80, 125, visit to Dalaradin,
  80 f; visits Tara, 88 ff; work
  in Connaught, 9, 25; tours
  through Ireland, 25; spreads
  knowledge of Latin, 21; alleged visit to Rome, 17; foundation of Armagh, 95 ff; date of
  his death, 1, 105; place of his
  death, 104; burial-place, 107,
  136 f

Peccator, as an epithet of Patrick, 110

Petitions of Patrick, 105, 135

Picts, 5, 54, 57, 58, 119, 123, 126

Potitus, grandfather of Patrick, 31, 73, 110

Probus (*Vita* v.), 8, 26, 70, 111, 113, 114 (*bis*)

Prosper of Aquitaine, 19, 122

Quadriga, name of Patrick, 110

Rathcrochan, 132

Relic, 133

Ridge of the Willow, 95, 131

Romani, 15 f, 119

Rome : Patrick desires to visit it, 76 ; his official connexion with Papal authorities, 16 ff ; alleged visit to, 17

Ronal. See Lucetmael

Rumili, bishop in Man, 94

Runtir, 124

Rusticus, 110

Sabhall Phadraig. See Saul

Sachellus, 17

Samhain, 127

Saul, 80, 104, 126, 136

Sayings of Patrick. See *Dicta Patricii*

Scadden, river, 126

Scirit *or* Scirte, mountain (Skerry), 81, 109, 126

Scotia (Ireland), 109

Scruple, 48, 117

Sechnall *or* Secundinus, 22 ; his Hymn, 22 ff, 105, 135 ; parallels with Patrick's writings, 116, 117 (*ter*), 118 (*bis*), 119 (*bis*) ; quoted by Muirchu, 71, 77, 80, 102, 123, 126, 134 ; other references, 120, 135

Sedulius quoted by Muirchu, 105, 135 f

Segitius, 77

Senchus Mór, 124, 128, 129

Skerries, 125

Skerry, mountain, 81, 109, 126

Slain, river, 80, 126

Slane, 86, 127

Slebte (Sletty), 71, 88, 101

Slemish, mountain. See Mis

Strangford Lough, 126, 130, 131

Sucat, name of Patrick, 73, 110

Sugere mammellas, 113 f

Sunday observed Sabbatically by Patrick, 97, 99, 103, 109

Tara. See Temoria

Tassach, 106, 136

Temoria, 78, 83 ff, 88, 92, 124, 129

Tempto, Patrick's use of, 115

Temro (Tara), 129

Tigris, sister of Patrick, 111

Tirechán's Memoir, 24 f, 68

Tirechán's Memoir, Extracts from (in Tirechán's order) :

Angelic visits on Skerry, 126

Summary of Patrick's travels, 11, 121 f

Patrick's landing in Ireland, 125 f

First meeting with Benignus, 129

Kannanus and the Easter Fire, 127

The magicians at Tara, 124

The ordeal by fire, 128 f

Death of Loch the magician, 128

Loiguire's profession of faith, 129

Conversion and baptism of Hercus, 127 f

Endeus from the Wood of Fochlath, 10

Patrick pays for travelling facilities, 117 f

Cry of the children of Fochlath, 10, 115

Conversion and death of Ethne and Fedelm, 132 f

Patrick at Rome, 17

Death and burial of Totmael the driver, 135

Vision of Saints on Croagh-Patrick, 8

Conversation with a dead heathen, 134

Tirechán's Memoir, other references, 9, 20, 113 (*bis*)
Todd, J. H., *Life of St. Patrick*, 27 f
Tonsure, 124 f, 133
Totmael the driver, 125, 134 f
Tripartite Life of Patrick, 26

Ui-Neill, 107, 108, 137
Ulaid *or* Ulidia, 80, 82, 92, 105, 108 (*bis*), 126
Ultao, 11, 14, 24

Vartry, river, 125
Ventre, 73, 111
Vergil quoted by Muirchu, 105, 135
Victoricus (man), 38, 115
Victoricus *or* Victor (angel), 73, 77, 81, 104, 106, 109, 126
Victorinus of Pettau, 12, 112, 113
Vitæ Patricii, 26
Vulgate, Patrick's acquaintance with, 2 ff

Whitby, synod of, 18

PUBLICATIONS

OF THE

S. P. C. K. &

THE SHELDON PRESS

BOOKS FOR

STUDENTS

AND

OTHERS

SOCIETY FOR PROMOTING CHRISTIAN KNOWLEDGE

AND

THE SHELDON PRESS

LONDON: NORTHUMBERLAND AVENUE, W.C. 2

BRIGHTON: 61 PRESTON STREET.   BATH: 39 GAY STREET

New York: THE MACMILLAN COMPANY

And of all Booksellers.

Translations of Early Documents (continued).

Midrash Sifre on Numbers. Selections from Early Rabbinic Scriptural Interpretations. Translated by PAUL P. LEVERTOFF. Introduction by Canon G. H. BOX, D.D. 7s. 6d.

Sukkah, Mishna and Tosefta. With Introduction, Translation and Short Notes by A. W. GREENUP, D.D. 5s.

Eusebius. Bishop of Cæsarea. The Ecclesiastical History and the Martyrs of Palestine. Translated, with Introduction and Notes, by HUGH JACKSON LAWLOR, D.D., Litt.D. and JOHN ERNEST LEONARD OULTON, B.D. Volume I. Translation Vol. II. Introduction, Notes and Appendix Each 10s. 6d.

Minucius Felix, and His Place among the Early Fathers of the Latin Church. By the Rev. HARRY JAMES BAYLIS, M.A., D.D. 15s.

Select Passages Illustrating Neoplatonism. Translated with an Introduction by E. R. DODDS, University College, Reading. 5s.

A Short Survey of the Literature of Rabbinical and Mediæval Judaism. By W. O. E. OESTERLEY, D.D., and G. H. BOX, D D. 12s. 6d.

Select Passages Illustrating Mithraism. With an Introduction by the Rev. A. S. GEDEN, D.D. 3s. 6d.

The Uncanonical Jewish Books A Short Introduction to the Apocrypha and the Jewish Writings 200 B.C.-A.D. 100. By W. JOHN FERRAR, M.A. 2s. 6d.

Barnabas, Hermas and the Didache Being the Donnellan Lectures, 1920, by J. ARMITAGE ROBINSON, D.D., Dean of Wells. 6s.

The Acts of the Apostles Translated from the Codex Bezae, with an Introduction on its Lucan Origin and importance by Canon J. M. WILSON, D.D. 3s. 6d.

Pistis Sophia Literally Translated from the Coptic by GEORGE HORNER. With an Introduction by F. LEGGE, F.S.A. 16s.

SERIES I.—GREEK TEXTS,

Justin Martyr. The Dialogue with Trypho. Translation, Introduction, and Notes by A. LUKYN WILLIAMS, D.D., Hon. Canon of Ely. 7s. 6d.

Selections from the Commentaries and Homilies of Origen. Translated by R. B. TOLLINTON, D.D. 10s.

The Ascetic Works of St. Basil. Translated into English, with Introduction and Notes, by W. K. L. CLARKE, D.D. 12s. 6d.

Dionysius the Areopagite: The Divine Names and the Mystical Theology. By C. E. ROLT. 7s. 6d.

The Library of Photius. By J. H. FREESE, M.A. Vol. I. 10s.

The Apocriticus of Macarius Magnes. By T. W. CRAFER, D.D. 7s. 6d.

The Epistle of St. Clement, Bishop of Rome. By the Most Rev. J. A. F. GREGG, D.D. 1s. 9d. (*Out of print.*)

Clement of Alexandria: Who is the Rich Man that is being saved ? By P. M. BARNARD, B.D. 1s. 9d.

St. Chrysostom: On the Priesthood. By T. A. MOXON. 4s. 6d.

The Doctrine of the Twelve Apostles. By C. BIGG, D.D. Revised by the Right Rev. A. J. MACLEAN, D.D. 3s. 6d.

The Epistle to Diognetus. By the Rt. Rev. L. B. RADFORD, D.D. 2s. 6d.

St. Dionysius of Alexandria. By C. L. FELTOE, D.D. 4s.

Translations of Christian Literature (continued).

SERIES I.—GREEK TEXTS (*continued*).

The Epistle of the Gallican Churches: Lugdunum and Vienna. With an Appendix containing Tertullian's Address to Martyrs and the Passion of St. Perpetua. By T. H. Bindley, D.D. *is. 9d.* (*Out of print.*)

St. Gregory of Nyssa: The Catechetical Oration. By the Ven. J. H. Srawley, D.D. *2s. 6d.*

St. Gregory of Nyssa: The Life of St. Macrina. By W. K. Lowther Clarke, D.D. *is. 9d.*

Gregory Thaumaturgus (Origen the Teacher): the Address of Gregory to Origen, with Origen's Letter to Gregory. By W. Metcalfe, B.D. *3s. 6d.*
[*Re-issue.*

The Shepherd of Hermas. By C. Taylor, D.D. 2 vols. *2s. 6d.* each.

Eusebius: The Proof of the Gospel. By W. J. Ferrar. 2 vols. *20s.* (*Not sold separately.*)

Hippolytus: Philosophumena. By F. Legge. 2 vols. *20s.* (*Not sold separately.*)

The Epistles of St. Ignatius. By the Ven. J. H. Srawley, D.D. *4s.*

St. Irenaeus: Against the Heresies. By F. R. M. Hitchcock, D.D. 2 vols. *2s. 6d.* each.

Palladius: The Lausiac History. By W. K. Lowther Clarke, D.D. *5s.*

The Dialogue of Palladius concerning the Life of Chrysostom. By Herbert Moore. *8s. 6d.*

Fifty Spiritual Homilies of St. Macarius the Egyptian. By A. J. Mason, D.D. *15s.*

SERIES II.—LATIN TEXTS.

St. Augustine on the Spirit and the Letter. By W. J. Sparrow Simpson, D.D. *5s.*

Tertullian's Treatises concerning Prayer, concerning Baptism. By A. Souter, D.Litt. *3s.*

Tertullian against Praxeas. By A. Souter, D.Litt. *5s.*

Translations of Christian Literature (continued).

SERIES II.—LATIN TEXTS (*continued*).

St. Bernard: The Twelve Degrees of Humility and Pride. Translated by BARTON R. V. MILLS, M.A. 6s. net.

Tertullian concerning the Resurrection of the Flesh. By A. SOUTER, D.Litt. 12s. 6d.

Tertullian: On the Testimony of the Soul and On the Prescription of Heretics. By T. H. BINDLEY, D.D. 2s. 6d.

Novatian on the Trinity. By H. MOORE. 6s.

St. Augustine: The City of God. By F. R. M. HITCH-COCK, D.D. Abridged. 3s.

St. Cyprian: The Lord's Prayer. By T. H. BINDLEY, D.D. 2s.

Minucius Felix: The Octavius. By J. H. FREESE. 3s. 6d.

St. Vincent of Lerins: The Commonitory. By T. H. BINDLEY, D.D. 2s. 6d.

St. Bernard: Concerning Grace and Free Will. By WATKIN W. WILLIAMS. 7s. 6d.

The Life of Otto: Apostle of Pomerania, 1060-1139. By EBO and HERBORDUS. Translated by CHARLES H. ROBINSON, D.D. 8s. 6d.

Select Epistles of St. Cyprian treating of the Episcopate. Edited with Introduction and Notes by T. A. LACEY, D.D. 8s. 6d.

Anskar, the Apostle of the North, 801–865. By CHARLES H. ROBINSON, D.D. Translated from the Vita Anskarii by BISHOP RIMBERT, his fellow-missionary and successor. 2s. 6d. [Published by S.P.G.]

SERIES III.—LITURGICAL TEXTS.

EDITED BY C. L. FELTOE, D.D.

Coptic Offices. Translated by REGINALD MAXWELL WOOLLEY, D.D. 6s.

St. Ambrose: On the Mysteries and on the Sacraments. By T. THOMPSON, B.D., and J. H. SRAWLEY, D.D. 4s. 6d.

The Apostolic Constitutions and Cognate Documents, with special reference to their Liturgical elements. By DE LACY O'LEARY, D.D. 1s. 9d.

13. **The French Renaissance.** By A. A. TILLEY, M.A. 8*d.*

14. **Hints on the Study of English Economic History.** By W. CUNNINGHAM, D.D., F.B.A., F.S.A. 8*d.*

15. **Parish History and Records.** By A. HAMILTON THOMPSON, M.A., F.S.A. 8*d.*

16. **A Short Introduction to the Study of Colonial History.** By A. P. NEWTON, M.A., D.Litt. 6*d.*

17. **The Wanderings and Homes of Manuscripts.** By M. R. JAMES, Litt.D., F.B.A. Paper, 2*s.*; cloth, 3*s.*

18. **Ecclesiastical Records.** By the Rev. Canon JENKINS, D.D. 1*s.* 9*d.*

19. **An Introduction to the History of American Diplomacy.** By CARL RUSSELL FISH, Ph.D. 1*s.*

20. **Hints on Translation from Latin into English.** By ALEXANDER SOUTER, D.Litt. 1*s.*

21. **Hints on the Study of Latin (A.D. 125-750).** By ALEXANDER SOUTER, D.Litt. 8*d.*

22. **Report of the Historical MSS. Commission.** By R. A. ROBERTS, F.R.Hist.S. 2*s.* 6*d.*

23. **A Guide to Franciscan Studies.** By A. G. LITTLE. 1*s.* 6*d.*

24. **A Guide to the History of Education.** By JOHN WILLIAM ADAMSON. 8*d.*

25. **Introduction to the Study of Russian History.** By W. F. REDDAWAY. 6*d.*

26. **Monuments of English Municipal Life.** By W. CUNNINGHAM, D.D., F.B.A. 1*s.*

27. **La Guyenne Pendant la Domination Anglaise, 1152-1453.** Par CHARLES BÉMONT. 1*s.* 4*d.*

28. **The Historical Criticism of Documents.** By R. L. MARSHALL, M.A., LL.D. 1*s.* 3*d.*

29. **The French Revolution.** By G. P. GOOCH. 8*d.*

30. **Seals.** By H. S. KINGSFORD. 1*s.* 3*d.*

31. **A Student's Guide to the Manuscripts of the British Museum.** By JULIUS P. GILSON, M.A. 1*s.*

32. **A Short Guide to some Manuscripts in the Library of Trinity College, Dublin.** By R. H. MURRAY, Litt.D. 1s. 9d.

33-35. **Ireland.** No. 33, 1494-1603; No. 34, 1603-1714; No. 35, 1714-1829. By R. H. MURRAY, Litt.D. Each, 1s. Nos. 33-35 in one volume, 3s. 6d.

36. **Coins and Medals.** By G. F. HILL, M.A., F.B.A. 1s. 6d.

37. **The Latin Orient.** By W. MILLER, M.A. 1s. 6d.

38. **The Turkish Restoration in Greece, 1718-1797.** By WILLIAM MILLER, M.A. 1s. 3d.

39. **Sources for the History of Roman Catholics in England, Ireland and Scotland, 1533-1795.** By JOHN HUNGERFORD POLLEN, S.J. 1s. 3d.

40. **English Time Books.—Vol. I. English Regnal Years and Titles, Hand-lists, Easter Dates, etc.** Compiled by J. E. W. WALLIS, M.A. 4s.

41. **Knights of Malta, 1523-1798.** By R. COHEN. 2s.

42. **Records for the Early History of South Africa.** By C. GRAHAM BOTHA. 1s.

43. **The Western Manuscripts of the Bodleian Library.** By H. H. E. CRASTER, D.Litt. 1s. 3d.

44. **Geographical Factors.** By H. J. FLEURE. 6d.

45. **The Colonial Entry Books. A Brief Guide to the Colonial Records in the Public Record Office before 1696.** By C. S. S. HIGHAM, M.A. 1s. 6d.

46. **The University Library, Cambridge.** By H. GIDNEY ALDIS, M.A. 6d.

47. **A Students' Guide to the Manuscripts relating to English History in the Seventeenth Century in the Bodleian Library.** By G. DAVIES. 1s.

48. **History and Ethnology.** By W. R. H. RIVERS, M.D., LL.D., F.R.S. 6d.

49. **Some Aspects of Boundary Settlement at the Peace Conference.** By ALAN G. OGILVIE, B.Sc. 6d.

50. **The Mechanical Processes of the Historian.** By CHARLES JOHNSON, M.A., F.S.A. 6d.

51. **The Sources for the History of the Council in the Sixteenth and Seventeenth Centuries.** E. R. ADAIR, M.A. 3s. 6d.

Texts for Students

1. **Select Passages from Josephus, Tacitus, Suetonius, Dio Cassius**, illustrative of Christianity in the First Century. Arranged by H. J. WHITE, D.D. *6d.*
2. **Selections from Matthew Paris.** By C. A. J. SKEEL, D.Lit. *9d.*
3. **Selections from Giraldus Cambrensis.** By C. A. J. SKEEL, D.Lit. *9d.*
4. **Libri Sancti Patricii.** The Latin Writings of St. Patrick, etc. By NEWPORT J. D. WHITE, D.D. *6d.*
5. **A Translation of the Latin Writings of St. Patrick.** By NEWPORT J. D. WHITE, D.D. *6d.*
6. **Selections from the Vulgate.** *9d.*
7. **The Epistle of St. Clement of Rome.** *6d.*
8. **Select Extracts from Chronicles and Records relating to English Towns in the Middle Ages.** By F. J. C. HEARNSHAW, M.A , LL.D. *9d.*
9. **The Inscription on the Stele of Méša.** Commonly called the Moabite Stone. Translated by the Rev. H. F. B. COMPSTON, M.A. *6d.*
10. **The Epistles of St. Ignatius.** *1s.*
11. **Christian Inscriptions.** By H. P. V. NUNN, M.A. *1s.*
12. **Selections from the "Historia Rerum Anglicarum"** of William of Newburgh. *1s. 3d.*
13. **The Teaching of the Twelve Apostles.** By T. W. CRAFER, D.D. *4d.* 13A. **An English Translation.** *3d.*
14. **The Epistle of Barnabas.** Edited by T. W. CRAFER, D D. *6d.* 14A. **An English Translation.** *6d.*
15. **The Code of Hammurabi.** By P. HANDCOCK, M.A. *1s.*
16. **Selections from the Tell El-Amarna Letters.** By PERCY HANDCOCK, M.A. *4d.*
17. **Select Passages Illustrating Commercial and Diplomatic Relations between England and Russia.** By A. WEINER, M.A., F.R.Hist.S. *1s. 6d.*
18. **The Early History of the Slavonic Settlements in Dalmatia, Croatia and Serbia.** By J. B. BURY. *2s.*
19. **Select Extracts Illustrating Florentine Life in the 13th and 14th Centuries.** By E. G. ROPER, B.A. *1s.*
20. **Select Extracts Illustrating Florentine Life in the 15th Century.** By ESTHER G. ROPER, B.A. *1s.*
    Nos. 19 and 20 in one volume, *2s. 6d.*
21. **Itinerarium Regis Ricardi.** By M. T. STEAD. *1s. 9d.*

22. **The Second Epistle of Clement to the Corinthians.**
    6*d.* 22A. **An English Translation.** 6*d.*

23. **Extracts Illustrating Sports and Pastimes in the Middle Ages.** By E. L. GUILFORD, M.A. 1*s.* 9*d.*

24. **Babylonian Flood Stories.** 25. **Babylonian Penitential Psalms.** By P. HANDCOCK, M.A. 6*d.* each.

26. **The Hymn of Cleanthes.** Translated with Introduction and Notes by E. H. BLAKENEY, M.A. 6*d.*

27. **The Foundations of Modern Ireland.** The Civil Policy of Henry VIII. and the Reformation. By CONSTANTIA MAXWELL, M.A. 1*s.* 6*d.*

28. **Selections from the Qur'án.** Arranged by H. U. WEITBRECHT STANTON, Ph.D., D.D. 1*s.*

29. **The Tome of Pope Leo the Great.** Latin Text with Translation, Introduction, and Notes, by E. H. BLAKENEY, M.A. 1*s.*; duxeen boards, 1*s.* 6*d.*

30. **The Book of Amos.** Hebrew Text edited by THEODORE H. ROBINSON, M.A., D.D. 2*s.* 6*d.*

31. **Sukkah. (A Critical Hebrew Text.)** By A. W. GREENUP, D.D. 2*s.* 6*d.*

32. **Readings from the Apocrypha.** Selected and Annotated by E. H. BLAKENEY, M.A. 1*s.*; cloth, 1*s.* 6*d.*

33 **English Social Life in the Eighteenth Century.**
& Illustrated from Contemporary Sources. By M. D.
34. GEORGE. Each 1*s.* 6*d.* In one vol., cloth, 3*s.* 6*d.*

35. **Texts Illustrating Ancient Ruler-Worship.** Edited by C. LATTEY, S.J., M.A. 6*d.*

35A. **An English Translation of the above.** 6*d.*

36. **Select Passages Illustrative of Neoplatonism.** Greek edition. Edited by E. R. DODDS, B.A. 4*s.* 6*d.*

37. **Traders in East and West.** Some Aspects of Trade in the 17th and 18th Centuries. By FLORENCE L. BOWMAN and ESTHER G. ROPER. 2*s.*

38. **Travellers and Travelling in the Middle Ages.** By E. L. GUILFORD, M.A. 2*s.*

39. **St. Augustine: De Fide et Symbolo.** Edited by HAROLD SMITH, D.D. 2*s.* 6*d.*

40. **God and His Works.** Being Selections from Part I. of the "Summa Theologica" of St. Thomas Aquinas. Arranged, with an Introduction, by A. G. HEBERT, M.A. Paper cover, 2*s.* 6*d.* Duxeen boards, 3*s.* 6*d.*

Texts for Students *(continued)*.

41. **Village Life in the Fifteenth Century.** Illustrated from Contemporary Sources by H. M. DUNCAN and W. J. HAWARD. *3s. 6d.*

42. **The Book of Ruth.** The Hebrew Text with Grammatical Notes and Vocabulary by A. R. S. KENNEDY, D.D. *2s. 6d.*

43. **Cyprian De Unitate Ecclesiæ.** The Latin text, translated, with an Introduction and Brief Notes, by E. H. BLAKENEY, M.A. *1s. 6d.*

44. **The Martyrdom of Polycarp.** Greek Text. *6d.*

45. **The Epistle to Diognetus.** Greek Text. *6d.*

The Bede Histories.

Edited by MISS H. L. POWELL, F.R.Hist.Soc.

SERIES III.

History of the People of England. By ALICE DRAYTON GREENWOOD, F.R.Hist.Soc. With many Maps and Illustrations.

Vol. I. 55 B.C. to A.D. 1485. *7s. 6d.*

History says. "The book is characterised by a general accuracy of detail."

Vol. II. 1485–1688. *7s. 6d.*

History says "Invaluable to the highest forms of schools and to undergraduates. . . One has the sense that everything is there which is wanted . . . a most useful instrument of teaching, not less to the teacher than the taught."

Vol. III. 1689–1834. *7s. 6d.*

The Times Literary Supplement says. "Fully maintains the high standard of the earlier volumes . . . should be of great value to the young University student. The facts are accurate, well co-ordinated and clearly set forth. . . . The maps, illustrations and reproductions are numerous and excellent."

Vol. IV. 1834–1910. *6s.*

SERIES II.

Vol. I. History of the People of England from the Earliest Times to 1066. By ADELINE I. RUSSELL, M.A. With 122 Illustrations and 8 Maps. *2s. 6d.*

The Teachers' Times says. ". . . Presented in a most attractive form. The outline is brightly written. . . . Incidents and quotations are taken, where possible, from contemporary authorities. Illustrations are very plentiful."

The Journal of Education says "Scholarly, well-balanced and thoroughly interesting."

Vol. III. The Tudors and Stuarts. By H. L. POWELL, F.R.Hist.Soc. With numerous Illustrations. *5s.*

The Times Educational Supplement says: "This book, like others in the same series, is attractively written and produced."

14

Studies in Church History

Richard Baxter. Puritan and Mystic. By A. R. LADELL, M.A. Preface by W. H. FRERE, D.D., Bishop of Truro. 5s.

The Dominican Order in England before the Reformation. By BERYL E. R. FORMOY, M.A. 6s.

The Cathedral Church of Hereford: Its History and Constitution. By ARTHUR THOMAS BANNISTER, M.A. 7s. 6d.

The Monastic Chronicler and the Early School of St. Albans. By Canon JENKINS, D.D. 3s. 6d.

The Christian Church in the Epistles of St. Jerome. By L. HUGHES, M.A., D.D. 4s. 6d.

The Prelude to the Reformation. By the Rev. R. S. ARROWSMITH. 8s.

The Albigensian Heresy. By H. J. WARNER, B.D. Vol. I. 3s. 6d. Vol. II. 6s.

The Early Franciscans and Jesuits. A Study in Contrasts. By ARTHUR S. B. FREER, M.A. 6s.

Some Eighteenth-Century Churchmen: Glimpses of English Church Life in the Eighteenth Century. By G. LACEY MAY, M.A. With Illustrations. 7s. 6d.

Christian Monasticism in Egypt to the Close of the Fourth Century. By W. H. MACKEAN, D.D. 8s.

The Venerable Bede. His Life and Writings. By the Rt. Rev. G. F. BROWNE, D.D. With Illustrations. 10s.

The Reformation in Ireland. A Study of Ecclesiastical Legislation. By H. HOLLOWAY, M.A. 7s. 6d.

The Emperor Julian. An Essay on His Relations with the Christian Religion. By EDWARD J. MARTIN, D.D. 3s. 6d.

The Importance of Women in Anglo-Saxon Times; The Cultus of St. Peter and St. Paul, and other Addresses. By the Right Rev. G. F. BROWNE, D.D. With two Illustrations. 7s. 6d.

French Catholics in the Nineteenth Century. By the Rev. W. J. SPARROW SIMPSON, D.D. 5s.

An Abbot of Vézelay. By ROSE GRAHAM, F.R.Hist.S. With eight Illustrations. 3s. 6d.

The Historic Monuments of England

Edited by A. HAMILTON THOMPSON, M.A. (Cantab.), Hon. D.Litt. (Durham), F.S.A., Professor of Mediæval History in the University of Leeds.

The Cathedral Churches of England. By A. HAMILTON THOMPSON, M.A., Hon. D.Litt. (Durham), F.S.A. With copious Illustrations. 8s. 6d.

Parish Church Architecture. By E. TYRRELL GREEN. With 64 Illustrations, chiefly from drawings by the Author, and a Map. 8s. 6d.

English Monumental Sculpture since the Renaissance. By KATHARINE A. ESDAILE. With many Illustrations. 10s. 6d.

The Painted Glass of York. An Account of the Mediæval Glass of the Minster and the Parish Churches. By the Rev. F. HARRISON, M.A., F.S.A., Librarian of the Dean and Chapter Library, York. With a Preface by W. FOXLEY NORRIS, D.D., Dean of Westminster. With four coloured Plates and numerous Illustrations. 12s. 6d.

English Mediæval Painted Glass. By J. D. LE COUTEUR. With about 50 Illustrations. 8s. 6d.

Sundials. Incised Dials and Mass-Clocks. A Study of the Time-Markers of Mediæval Churches, containing Descriptions, Photographs, Diagrams, and Analysis of Dials, chiefly in Hampshire, but also in various other counties By ARTHUR ROBERT GREEN, M.R.C.S. (England), L.R.C.P. (London). 10s. 6d.

Baptismal Fonts. Classified and Illustrated. By E. TYRRELL GREEN. With over 100 Illustrations. 10s. 6d.

French Church Architecture. By E. TYRRELL GREEN. With about 70 Illustrations. 10s. 6d. net.

[1.12.32.

Printed in Great Britain by R. Clay & Sons, Ltd., Bungay, Suffolk.